PSYCHOSOMATIC
DISORDERS

Theoretical and Clinical Aspects

D0145593

BRUNNER/MAZEL
BASIC PRINCIPLES INTO PRACTICE SERIES
Series Editor: Natalie H. Gilman

The *Brunner/Mazel Basic Principles Into Practice Series* is designed to present—in a series of concisely written, easily understandable volumes—the basic theory and clinical principles associated with a variety of disciplines and types of therapy. These volumes will serve not only as "refreshers" for practicing therapists, but also as basic texts on the college and graduate level.

7. Psychosomatic Disorders: Theoretical and Clinical Aspects
   By Ghazi Asaad, M.D.

6. Therapy With Stepfamilies
   By Emily B. Visher, Ph.D., and John S. Visher, M.D.

5. Psychotherapeutic Metaphors: A Guide to Theory and Practice
   By Philip Barker

4. Essentials of Hypnosis
   By Michael D. Yapko, Ph.D.

3. Understanding Mental Disorders Due to Medical Conditions or Substance Abuse: What Every Therapist Should Know
   By Ghazi Asaad, M.D.

2. Essentials of Psychoanalysis
   By Herbert S. Strean, D.S.W.

1. Family Therapy: Fundamentals of Theory and Practice
   By William A. Griffin, Ph.D.

1993

BRUNNER/MAZEL
BASIC PRINCIPLES INTO PRACTICE SERIES
VOLUME 7

PSYCHOSOMATIC DISORDERS

Theoretical and Clinical Aspects

GHAZI ASAAD, M.D.

DREXEL UNIVERSITY
HEALTH SCIENCES LIBRARIES
HAHNEMANN LIBRARY

BRUNNER/MAZEL, *Publishers* • NEW YORK

WM
90
A798p
1996

Library of Congress Cataloging-in-Publication Data

Asaad, Ghazi.
  Psychosomatic disorders: theoretical and clinical aspects / Ghazi
Asaad.
    p.   cm. — (Brunner/Mazel basic principles into practice series; v. 7)
  Includes bibliographical references and index.
  ISBN 0-87630-803-5
  1. Medicine, Psychosomatic. 2. Somatoform disorders. I. Title.
II. Series.
RC49.A75   1996
616.08—dc20
                                                                96-7078
                                                                     CIP

Copyright © 1996 by Brunner/Mazel, Inc.

All rights reserved. No part of this book may
be reproduced by any process whatsoever without
the written permission of the copyright owner.

Published by
BRUNNER/MAZEL, INC.
19 Union Square West
New York, New York 10003

Manufactured in the United States of America
      10   9   8   7   6   5   4   3   2   1

To Dena, Nadine, Samer, and Mazen,
my wonderful children
with love...

CONTENTS

Introduction ix

PART I: SOMATOFORM DISORDERS 1

1. Somatization Disorder 3
2. Conversion Disorder 11
3. Hypochondriasis 19
4. Body Dysmorphic Disorder 27
5. Pain Disorder 33

**PART II: FACTITIOUS DISORDERS
AND MALINGERING** 43

6. Factitious Disorder with Physical Signs
   and Symptoms 45
7. Factitious Disorder with Psychological
   Signs and Symptoms 53
8. Malingering 59

**PART III: MEDICAL CONDITIONS AFFECTED
    BY PSYCHOLOGICAL FACTORS 63**

9.   Gastrointestinal Disorders Affected by
     Psychological Factors 65

10. Cardiovascular Disorders Affected by
     Psychological Factors 77

11. Respiratory Disorders Affected by
     Psychological Factors 83

12. Dermatological Disorders Affected by
     Psychological Factors 91

13. The Role of Psychological Factors in
     Immune Disorders and Cancer 95

14. Psychological Factors Affecting
     Headaches and Migraine 101

15. The Role of Psychological Factors
     in Obesity 107

16. Fibromyalgia 113

17. Chronic Fatigue Syndrome 119

18. Premenstrual Syndrome 125

19. Future Direction of Psychosomatic
     Medicine 129

     References 133
     Name Index 141
     Subject Index 145

INTRODUCTION

The mind–body connection has fascinated clinicians and researchers for centuries. In prehistoric times, there was the belief that disease was caused by evil spirits and illness could be cured by exorcism and trepanation. People of ancient civilizations believed that the mind had great power over the body and that the body could not be cured without curing the head. During the Middle Ages, mysticism and religious influences dominated medicine and reinforced the beliefs that physical illness could be caused by psychic power. The understanding of the relationship between the mind and the body continued to evolve during the centuries that followed, especially during the latter part of the 19th century and the 20th century. The psychoanalytic formulations presented by Freud in an attempt to understand the concept of hysteria led the way for others to explore the mysteries of the interactive relationship between the mind and the body. Modern research and advanced diagnostic tools have been able to identify specific neurochemical and hormonal mechanisms that can account for some physical conditions that are affected by psychological factors and for psychological symptoms that are caused by medical conditions (Asaad, 1995).

Illnesses that appear to be caused by physical disorders may in fact be due to psychological factors, as in the cases of hysterical paralysis and Somatization Disorder. Conversely, certain medical conditions may present with various behavioral changes and psychological symptoms, as in the cases of vitamin deficiency and traumatic brain injuries. Furthermore, many medical illnesses can be heavily influenced by psychological factors, leading to further complications or improvement, as in peptic ulcers and headaches.

The relationship between physical conditions and psychological factors is not fully understood. Although it has been agreed that unconscious conflicts and psychosocial stressors are at the heart of that relationship, no specific causal relationship has yet been established in that regard. Recent developments in the field of neuropsychiatry, along with advances in the fields of endocrinology and immunology, have provided more convincing arguments in support of various theories and hypotheses. It is believed that psychological processes are mediated via various neurotransmitter systems, which in turn influence the endocrine and immune systems, causing the emergence of certain physical symptoms. Conversely, physical factors that disrupt the endocrine or other chemical systems are likely to affect several neurotransmitter systems, leading to a variety of psychological manifestations. The exact role of the immune system in this entire process remains unclear; however, it is likely that plasma cells, lymphocytes and immunoglobulins interact mutually with both endocrine and neurotransmitter systems.

This discussion of Psychosomatic and Somatoform Disorders attempts to bridge the gap between the mind and the body and to integrate various factors that are involved in many conditions that lie at the border between medicine and psychiatry. The first section of the book discusses Somatoform Disorders; these include Somatization Disorder, Conversion Disorder, hypochondriasis, Body Dysmorphic Disorder, and Pain Disorder. The essence of this category is that the presenting physical complaint cannot be explained by any known medical condition. Patients are always convinced that their illness is of a physical nature, undergo extensive and costly diagnostic procedures, and often refuse to accept psychological treatments.

Factitious Disorders refer to physical or psychological symptoms that are intentionally produced in order to assume the sick role without any obvious secondary gains. This is in contrast to malingering, in which secondary gain is obvious. These categories are presented in the second section of this book. Patients with Factitious Disorders are likely to be seen by numerous health care providers and to visit many emergency rooms, presenting with multiple physical or psychological complaints that cannot be substantiated by examinations or other objective diagnostic tools.

The last section of this book deals with various physical syndromes that are either caused or aggravated by psychological factors. Examples include irritable bowel syndrome and hypertension. The section encompasses a group of disorders that manifest with physical as well as psychological symptoms, and seem to be caused by a combination of physical and psychological factors. Examples include chronic fatigue syndrome and premenstrual syndrome. In the section "Psychological Factors Affecting Medical Conditions," DSM-IV (1994) lists a variety of psychiatric conditions that tend to adversely affect the general medical condition. They include major psychiatric syndromes, Personality Disorders, maladaptive health behavior, stressful circumstances, and other psychological factors. Although any medical condition can be affected by psychological factors, the disorders discussed in this last section have been shown to be most influenced by such factors.

Patients with Somatoform and Factitious Disorders and those with certain physical illnesses that can be aggravated by emotional stress are likely to wander from doctor to doctor and from one hospital to another in search of answers for their mysterious illnesses and an ultimate cure, which does not seem to come. Such patients tend to exhaust medical resources and utilize a great deal of health care services and diagnostic procedures, which often prove fruitless. These patients are typically skeptical about mental health professionals and are unlikely to consent to psychological evaluation or treatment. This book is designed to help identify such patients and to show how to work with them effectively in collaboration with other medical providers. It is intended for psychotherapists of all backgrounds and for graduate students of various psychology and social work programs. In many ways, it complements my other book in this series, *Understanding Mental Disorders Due to Medical Conditions or Substance Abuse: What Every Therapist Should Know* (Asaad, 1995). Both books examine interface issues between medicine and psychiatry in a way that is accessible to readers without medical training. I have presented several clinical vignettes in order to clarify certain conditions, and I have attempted to simplify the medical language and terminology as much as possible in order to make the material beneficial to the diverse readership of mental health professionals. Names and identities of patients reported in the case examples have been altered in order to protect patient confidentiality.

Part I

Somatoform Disorders

1

SOMATIZATION DISORDER

DEFINITION AND CLINICAL PRESENTATION

Somatization Disorder refers to recurrent multiple physical symptoms and complaints that cannot be substantiated or explained on the basis of known medical conditions despite repeated physical examinations and extensive diagnostic investigations. Consequently, it is presumed that the symptoms are not caused by a general medical condition or a drug. Usually, patients who suffer from Somatization Disorder are otherwise healthy; however, the condition can arise in medically ill individuals. In such patients, the clinical presentation of the medical condition is grossly exaggerated and many of the stated complaints cannot be explained on the basis of objective findings. The somatic complaints in the course of Somatization Disorder are usually of sufficient severity to warrant the pursuit of medical treatment or to impair social or occupational functioning. The disorder occurs mostly in women and in relatively young people (before age 30), and assumes a chronic course of variable severity and fluctuation. The somatic complaints are typically numerous, exaggerated, and colorful, and the patient is often inconsistent in her or his description.

3

For this diagnosis to be made, DSM-IV (1994) requires the presence of several symptoms in four major categories:

1. Four pain symptoms related to the head, abdomen, pelvis, back, joints, or other areas.
2. Two gastrointestinal symptoms, such as nausea, bloating, vomiting, diarrhea, or intolerance to various foods.
3. One sexual symptom, such as sexual indifference, erectile or ejaculatory dysfunction, irregular menses, or excessive menstrual bleeding.
4. One pseudoneurological symptom, such as paralysis or numbness, impaired coordination or loss of balance, difficulty swallowing, loss of voice, visual or auditory deficits, seizures, loss of consciousness, amnesia, or hallucinations.

Patients are known for seeking treatment from several physicians in an attempt to uncover the "mystery of their physical ailment." They may be reassured by the negative outcome of the investigations only to return with a new set of complaints or to experience the "recurrence" of their original symptoms shortly thereafter. Patients tend to seek hospitalization and expensive diagnostic investigations, and may consent to major invasive procedures, including surgery.

ASSOCIATED FEATURES

Many patients present with several psychiatric symptoms, including depression, anxiety, insomnia, and suicidal behavior. Such symptoms may be severe enough to warrant a separate diagnosis. Several Personality Disorders or traits are commonly encountered in the course of this disorder, including Histrionic, Borderline, and Antisocial Personality Disorders. Some patients tend to abuse alcohol or prescription drugs, such as painkillers and anxiolytic agents. It is fairly common to observe serious marital and family problems among patients with Somatization Disorder. The patient's job or school performance declines due to repeated absences and anxiety or preoccupation with various health issues. Occasionally, the patient may present with a genuine medical illness prior to or during the course of Somatization Disorder. In such instances, the somatic complaints are far beyond the expected actual manifestations of the medical illness as evidenced by physical examination and laboratory investigations. At times, side effects of unnecessarily prescribed medications and complications resulting from invasive procedures or surgery can lead to serious medical problems.

Case Example

Heather was a 34-year-old woman who reluctantly came to the psychiatrist's office after being referred repeatedly by her primary care physician. The patient had been seen by numerous specialists over the preceding seven years for multiple somatic complaints. She protested the need to see the psychiatrist and affirmed, "I am not crazy and all these medical problems are real and not just in my head." She complained of headache, dizziness, difficulty swallowing, diffuse abdominal pain, bloating, diarrhea, back pain, severe menstrual cramps, and loss of sexual interest. She said that her marriage was in trouble and that her husband was fed up with her "medical problems" and all the bills that they had to pay. She was unable to keep a job because she was always in pain and had to take long sick leaves. Over the past seven years, she had to change doctors many times because they could not find out what was causing her symptoms. She had numerous X rays, CT scans, MRIs, and blood tests; none of which showed any abnormal results. She added, "One time, the surgeon had to go in to find out, but everything was OK." "Doctor, you have to believe me, the pain is real, all the symptoms are real, I am not making this up," she cried. She pointed to a bag full of prescription drugs: "These medications don't

help; I don't know what to do." "Yes, I am depressed, and
I am angry, and sometimes I think it is better to be dead
than to live like this," she added in a faint voice. The
patient then began to cry, "I am sorry Doctor, but can you
really help me?"

Heather represents a typical patient with Somatization
Disorder which, like most Somatoform Disorders, is seen
more often in medical settings than in psychiatric practices; except during later stages when medical specialists
refuse to perform any further investigations or treatments.
Heather agreed to work with the psychiatrist and was seen
in psychotherapy for several months and was given an
antidepressant medication. The therapeutic techniques
used during the course of her treatment involved listening
to her lengthy complaints, acknowledging her distress,
and identifying areas of psychopathology that could have
contributed to her difficulties. Although she continued to
experience many of her original symptoms, she was able to
cope with her problems. Her visits to various doctors
diminished significantly and her marital life improved.
The patient kept in frequent contact with the psychiatrist
and her primary care physician and was able to maintain
her improvement over the following two years.

ETIOLOGY AND CONTRIBUTING FACTORS

Little is known about the causes of Somatization Disorder,
however, several theories have been proposed. Kellner
(1991) reviewed such theories, citing genetic, psychiatric,
physiological, behavioral and psychodynamic factors.
Adoption studies have shown that some patients exhibit
certain psychopathology in the area of Somatization Disorder similar to that found in their biological parents.
These findings suggest that genetic factors play an important role in certain somatization syndromes.

While the exact relationship between Somatization Disorder and depression is not fully understood, it has been

shown through research and in clinical practice that depressed patients tend to have more somatic complaints than do nondepressed individuals. Conversely, patients who suffer from Somatization Disorder have a much higher incidence of depression as compared with patients with actual physical illnesses. Like depression, anxiety appears to be highly associated with Somatization Disorder.

Several physiological dysfunctions have also been implicated as contributing factors to Somatization Disorder. These include abnormalities in smooth or striated muscle contraction, changes in blood flow and endocrine secretion, variations in physiological arousal, and low pain threshold.

Other theories have proposed that Somatization Disorder may be understood as learned abnormal perceptions or as a cognitive style. These mechanisms may be heavily influenced by childhood experiences and by events occurring during adult life.

Psychodynamic factors provide the most interesting frame for thinking in the attempt to understand the drive behind somatic symptoms. These factors include repressed hostility, anger, attention seeking, secondary gain, suppression of emotions, alexithymia (inability to express emotions), and using bodily metaphors to communicate an unconscious conflict or express emotional distress.

DIAGNOSIS AND DIFFERENTIAL DIAGNOSIS

The essential feature of Somatization Disorder is the early onset of chronic multiple somatic complaints that cannot be substantiated by physical examinations or diagnostic investigations. The condition may need to be differentiated from various medical illnesses, major depression, Panic Disorder, hypochondriasis, Factitious Disorder, and malingering.

Reasonable physical examinations and appropriate diagnostic investigations need to be performed. It is essen-

tial to emphasize here that actual physical illnesses may
occur concurrently with Somatization Disorder and should
be treated independently. More important, physical complaints made by somatic patients need to be assessed
carefully since there is always the chance that the symptoms are genuine. In fact, many actual physical illnesses
may go undiagnosed for a long time in such patients
because of the assumption that the symptoms are part of
the psychosomatic syndrome.

In major depression, somatic symptoms can be numerous and may not be explained on the basis of any physical
condition. The presence of typical symptoms of major
depression and the relative quick resolution of somatic
complaints as the depression lifts may aid in distinguishing the two conditions. It must also be kept in mind that
depressive symptoms can coexist with Somatization Disorder in which case both diagnoses should be made.

Panic Disorder can present with multiple somatic symptoms that cannot be substantiated on the basis of any
medical condition. As in the case of depression, Anxiety
and Panic Disorders can occur simultaneously with
Somatization Disorder, in which case both diagnoses can
be made.

In hypochondriasis, the patient is preoccupied with his
or her health and may be afraid of various diseases.
Occasionally, the patient may present with several so-
matic complaints that can mimic Somatization Disorder.
However, it must be kept in mind that patients with
Somatization Disorder may present with other Somatoform
Disorders, including hypochondriasis, at the same time.

In Factitious Disorder with predominant physical features, the patient may present with psychosomatic symptoms. However, the symptoms are usually few and the
patient shows inappropriate affect in proportion to his or
her degree of alleged physical distress. The drive behind
the symptoms here is for the patient to assume the sick
role.

In malingering, the patient is often motivated by a
secondary gain and the complaints are often inconsistent.

Cases that do not meet the diagnostic criteria for Somatization Disorder proposed by DSM-IV (1994), including those where the number of symptoms is limited, the age of onset is later in life, or the condition does not take a chronic course, may be classified under "Undifferentiated Somatoform Disorder."

TREATMENT APPROACHES

Patients with Somatization Disorder rarely agree to see a mental health professional because of their firm belief that their symptoms are physical in nature and that there is nothing emotionally wrong with them. They are often referred by physicians who no longer agree to investigate or treat their complaints. A spouse or other family member often pressures the patient to seek psychiatric care.

The patient will never agree with the therapist that the symptoms are caused by psychological factors, at least initially. Therefore, the therapist must listen with empathy to the lengthy list of physical complaints and acknowledge the distress that is endured by the patient. The therapist should attempt to identify stressors that may precede the onset of somatic symptoms and help the patient develop strategies to deal with the stressors effectively and to learn how to cope with the physical distress. While the therapist should not agree with the patient's convictions, he or she must not oppose them. The therapist should in fact allow the patient to have limited contact with his or her primary care physician on a regular basis and have scheduled appointments with limited access to diagnostic procedures. This technique will provide the patient with adequate reassurance, allowing the therapist to establish the therapeutic alliance that will eventually facilitate the identification and resolution of psychological conflicts. As the therapeutic process evolves, the therapist will be able to identify areas of psychopathology in the patient's life that may be linked somehow to the somatic problems. The patient's resistance to such interpretations should be expected and acknowledged in order to keep the patient engaged in treatment. Later on, the therapist may be able to make effective interpretations. Regular communication between the therapist and the primary care physician is vital if treatment is to succeed.

Psychotherapeutic techniques utilized in the treatment of Somatization Disorder must remain eclectic and flexible. Supportive, cognitive, behavioral, and insight-oriented psychotherapies may be used. Biofeedback and relaxation techniques are helpful in certain cases.

Smith, Monson, and Ray (1986) suggested that some patients may be managed better by their primary care physician, who, in consultation with the psychiatrist, will agree to see the patient on a regular basis (every four to six weeks) for physical examination and reassurance as long as hospitalization and diagnostic procedures are avoided unless clearly indicated.

Psychopharmacological interventions may be useful, especially when depression, anxiety, or panic symptoms coexist with Somatization Disorder. Antidepressants, anxiolytics, and other psychotropic medications may be used, depending on the clinical presentation.

COURSE AND PROGNOSIS

Somatization Disorder tends to assume a chronic course, with periods of increased severity and other periods of relative remission. As indicated previously, some patients may suffer from complications resulting from unwarranted invasive diagnostic procedures, surgeries, and drug therapies. In addition, many patients suffer a great deal of disruption in their occupational and family life.

Although complete resolution of Somatization Disorder is rare, partial remission through the use of the treatment approach outlined above is possible.

2

CONVERSION DISORDER

DEFINITION AND CLINICAL PRESENTATION

Conversion Disorder may be defined as a Somatoform Disorder in which the patient may exhibit certain symptoms or deficits involving motor or sensory functions that cannot be substantiated on the basis of physical examination or diagnostic procedures. The symptoms are generally associated with psychological conflicts or stressors and are not under the voluntary control of the patient. Usually, the symptoms or deficits are significant enough to interfere with the patient's social or occupational functioning. Unlike Somatization Disorder, Conversion Disorder may involve a single symptom, with the exception of pain or sexual dysfunction, which may be classified under different categories (DSM-IV, 1994).

DSM-IV (1994) proposes four subtypes of Conversion Disorder:

- Conversion Disorder with motor symptoms or deficits, which includes paralysis, weakness, difficulty swallowing, aphonia (loss of voice), and urinary retention.
- Conversion Disorder with sensory symptoms or deficits, which includes loss of sensation, double vision, blindness, deafness, and hallucinations.
- Conversion Disorder with seizures or convulsions

(pseudoseizures), which involves motor or sensory components.
- Conversion Disorder with mixed perceptions. This subtype refers to Conversion Disorder that involves more than one category of symptoms or deficits.

The disorder occurs more often in women than in men and starts in early adulthood, although Conversion Disorders have been reported in both children and geriatric patients. It has been reported to be more common in rural areas and in populations of lower socioeconomic status. In addition, there is some evidence to suggest that conversion symptoms are more frequent in relatives of individuals with Conversion Disorder (DSM-IV, 1994).

Although Conversion Disorder usually signifies the absence of physical illness, it is fairly common to see in various medical practices a large number of patients presenting with Conversion Disorder as a hysterical exacerbation of an actual somatic illness (Merskey, 1989). Examples include the onset of severe dizziness and incoordination of muscle movement following mild head injury and the onset of persistent difficulty in swallowing (globus hystericus) following the recovery from ordinary throat infection.

ASSOCIATED FEATURES

Other psychiatric symptoms or disorders may be associated with Conversion Disorder, including major depression, schizophrenia, Dissociative Disorder, and other Somatoform Disorders. In addition, Conversion Disorder seems to occur more often in patients with histrionic, dependent, or antisocial personality organization.

Case Example

Laura, a 23-year-old college student, was admitted to the neurological service to investigate a sudden onset of paralysis involving both legs. There was no history of trauma or infection. Physical examination was completely normal, revealing normal reflexes and sensory functions of both legs. There was no evidence for vascular or muscular disease. Complete laboratory investigations and MRI of the brain and spinal cord showed no abnormalities. A psychiatric consultation was requested. The patient was sitting in her bed smiling, and as the psychiatrist approached, she greeted him with a skeptical look. "I don't know how to make you doctors believe that I honestly cannot move my legs," she said. "I am not making this up. I am missing my final exams. I am supposed to get married next month. Everything is going well for me. Why would I want to ruin everything?" she added angrily. Laura proceeded to talk about the onset of her symptoms. With a superficial smile, she said, "My family is very upset. Jeff is extremely concerned. And I don't know where this problem came from; I just want to walk again."

Laura had to be released from the hospital as there were no medical reasons to require hospital care. She reluctantly agreed to see the psychiatrist, and each week was brought to the office in a wheelchair. A history revealed that the patient had met Jeff a year earlier and had fallen in love with him instantly. "My family, which is very strict, liked him, and everyone said that we were perfect for each other," she said. Laura told the psychiatrist how Jeff proposed to her: "It was the best moment in my life." In the following sessions, she related minor incidents where Jeff lost his temper. "He seemed like a different person," she said. During another session, she recalled, "He drank too much and was flirting with my girlfriend," adding in a doubtful voice, "I guess he will be all right; nobody is perfect." As the treatment progressed, Laura was able to express her concerns about the relationship and that her decision to get married might have been premature. Several weeks into her treatment, she began to report some improvement in muscle movement in both of her legs, and one day she came into the office using a walker. "See, Doc, I think I am getting better," she stated with confidence.

And she did. Her motor functions continued to improve over the next several weeks until she returned to her normal strength. During one of her final therapy sessions she announced cheerfully, "Guess what, it is over. Jeff is gone."

In Laura's case, it was clear that her unconscious conflict about getting married to Jeff had been behind the emergence of the paralysis, symbolizing her reluctance to go ahead with the plan. Bringing the conflict into consciousness allowed the patient to express her anxiety and fear and to work them through in therapy, which resulted in the eventual disappearance of the paralysis.

ETIOLOGY AND CONTRIBUTING FACTORS

It has long been accepted by clinicians and writers that the essential mechanism in Conversion Disorder is the "conversion" of an unconscious psychological conflict into a somatic symptom or deficit for the purpose of avoiding severe anxiety. This may be considered as a primary gain about which the patient is usually unconscious. The patient may also be unconsciously seeking secondary gain where the "physical" condition allows him or her to receive attention and special treatment.

Merskey (1989) outlined several contributing factors to Conversion Disorder, including the patient's attempt to attract attention; severe Personality Disorders, such as histrionic and antisocial personalities; a history of childhood deprivation and abuse; severe stress; and psychiatric disorders, such as depression and schizophrenia.

Slater (1965) reported that damage to the brain or intoxication with certain drugs, such as anticonvulsants, may predispose patients to experience conversion symptoms. Kellner (1991) concluded on the basis of several experiments and psychophysiological research conducted by others that patients with Conversion Disorder are physiologically different from healthy individuals and other "neurotic" patients. He suggested that such patients show high levels of arousal, habituate or react slowly to stress, and have lower sensitivity to somatosensory stimuli.

It has been documented that conversion symptoms and other somatoform symptoms can occur as part of an epidemic (mass hysteria). Conversion Disorder can also occur in otherwise healthy individuals subjected to overwhelming unbearable stress. Unlike Somatization Disorder, Conversion Disorder has no significant genetic contribution (Kellner, 1991).

DIAGNOSIS AND DIFFERENTIAL DIAGNOSIS

Conversion Disorder should only be considered after all physical examinations and diagnostic investigations have been exhausted and have proved negative. Even then, one must keep in mind that certain medical conditions may present with vague and unusual symptoms and may take months or years to be documented, for example—multiple sclerosis and myasthenia gravis. It is important to emphasize, however, that the presence of a medical problem does not preclude Conversion Disorder, as the conditions can coexist.

Patients with Conversion Disorder often exhibit a relative lack of concern about the perceived "serious illness," a phenomenon known as "la belle indifference." Or, as in Somatization Disorder, they may be highly emotional, dramatic, and colorful. They are often inconsistent in their description of symptoms and may be able to perform certain tasks that patients with genuine deficits are unable to perform. The symptoms often do not follow anatomical or physiological pathways; rather, they conform to the patient's own perception of the condition. For example, patients with conversion anesthesia in the hand will report loss of sensation in the entire hand from the wrist down while sensation is normal above the wrist (glove and stocking anesthesia). This, of course, is anatomically impossible since nerve distribution follows different pathways. Patients with hysterical seizures (pseudoseizures) rarely injure themselves when they fall, and EEG tracings even during the "seizure" are normal.

It is important to look for a connection between the symptom or deficit and any psychological conflict or stressor. A detailed psychosocial history is essential in the process of making this diagnosis. Psychological tests have not been shown to be helpful in the understanding or diagnosis of Conversion Disorder, perhaps because of the diverse psychological profiles and personality organizations of patients who present with the disorder (Kellner, 1991).

In some developing cultures, conversion symptoms may be viewed as acceptable and credible ways to express distress. Furthermore, certain forms of conversion symptoms as well as dissociative states can be present as common aspects of culturally sanctioned religious and healing rituals. Therefore, DSM-IV (1994) recommends that a diagnosis of Conversion Disorder should not be made if the condition can be explained on the basis of cultural or religious grounds.

Conversion Disorder needs to be differentiated from general medical conditions, major depression, schizophrenia, Factitious Disorder, and malingering. General medical conditions can be ruled out on the basis of physical examination and diagnostic investigations.

In major depression, some patients may present with certain somatic complaints that can not be substantiated. In such instances, the presence of depressive symptoms may facilitate the diagnosis. However, and as indicated earlier, Conversion Disorder and depression can coexist, in which case both diagnoses should be made.

In schizophrenia, patients with somatic delusions may describe somatic symptoms that cannot be explained on the basis of a known medical illness. Furthermore, Conversion Disorder may take the form of auditory or visual hallucinations (Asaad, 1990). History, level of functioning, and the presence or absence of schizophrenic symptoms can help distinguish between the two conditions.

In Factitious Disorder with predominantly somatic symptoms, somatic complaints may present like conversion symptoms; however, in Factitious Disorder, the patient often induces or causes the symptoms for the purpose of assuming the sick role.

In malingering, the patient is clearly motivated by secondary gain and the symptoms are within the full control of the patient.

TREATMENT APPROACHES

The focus of treatment should be on removing the somatic problem and addressing the patient's psychological conflicts and interpersonal or social maladjustment. Any coexisting medical condition needs to be treated promptly. Other psychiatric symptoms should be dealt with effectively, and appropriate psychotropic medications may be given. Various psychotherapeutic techniques may be employed, including the power of suggestion, hypnosis, psychoanalysis, insight-oriented psychotherapy, supportive psychotherapy, behavioral therapy, and family and social support (Merskey, 1989).

During the course of treatment it is essential to provide the patient with maximum reassurance and psychological support in addition to attempting to lower the level of stress.

COURSE AND PROGNOSIS

The onset of Conversion Disorder is typically acute and often occurs in connection with a psychological conflict or stressor. In most instances, the duration of the condition is brief, and most symptoms resolve following appropriate psychological intervention. However, in some cases, the course can be lengthy and the disorder becomes chronic;

in others, remission may be followed by cycles of relapse and remission for some time. It is likely that Conversion Disorder will resolve in response to treatment at some point, but it is possible that a genuine medical disorder can develop in the meantime, which may be perceived as another conversion condition.

Generally, cases that occur acutely under severe stress, especially in younger patients, have a better prognosis. The presence of other psychiatric disorders and Personality Disorders may complicate the recovery.

3

HYPOCHONDRIASIS

DEFINITION AND CLINICAL PRESENTATION

The term "hypochondriasis" derives from the Greek belief that the syndrome was caused by disturbances of the viscera below the xiphoid cartilage (Martin & Yutzy, 1994). Hypochondriasis may be defined as excessive preoccupation with fear of disease or strong belief in having disease on the basis of false interpretation of trivial physical signs or symptoms. Such preoccupation is usually unfounded and cannot be substantiated by complete physical examination and appropriate diagnostic procedures. The patient may start out with a transient thought concerning a specific disease following media coverage of it or upon hearing of someone who was diagnosed with the condition. Gradually, the patient begins to experience feelings that suggest to him or her that he or she has the same disease. Often, the patient will look for signs in support of this belief, eventually building a strong case in his or her own mind. The patient then tells family members and proceeds to see various doctors, seeking multiple diagnostic investigations. Most often, the patient will not be reassured by negative physical examination and laboratory investigations. However, some patients may agree with the physician that they may be exaggerating the extent of the feared disease, or that there may not be a disease at all. Such reassurance is usually short lived, and the patient soon returns to the hypochondriacal state, coming up with a new set of reasons in support of his or her conviction and explaining why the investigations had failed to document the disease. Occasionally, patients will generate a different set of symptoms indicating another disease and go through the same cycle again. Generally, the false beliefs do not reach a delusional level, but, in many patients, it is fairly difficult to shake them.

Another variety of hypochondriasis involves patients with ordinary physical illnesses who believe that their illnesses are in fact serious or terminal. A patient with a breast mass may believe that the tumor is malignant despite a biopsy report to the contrary or a patient may believe that he has AIDS based on experiencing recurrent respiratory infections and skin rashes.

The disease affects men and women equally and seems to strike most commonly during early adulthood. The prevalence in general medical practices ranges between 4 percent and 9 percent. The onset is usually sudden and may be preceded by a psychological stress, particularly the death of someone close. The course is chronic, with waxing and waning symptoms. DSM-IV (1994) requires that the symptoms persist for at least six months for the diagnosis to be made, and recommends distinguishing the disorder from other transient or less significant conditions which may not qualify for the diagnosis of hypochondriasis. Furthermore, the DSM-IV (1994) advises that the diagnosis should not be made if symptoms arise in the course of Generalized Anxiety Disorder, Obsessive-Compulsive Disorder, Panic Disorder, major depression, separation anxiety, or another Somatoform Disorder.

ASSOCIATED FEATURES

Hypochondriasis is often associated with severe anxiety symptoms. Frequently, depressive symptoms are observed, especially in chronic cases. It is not uncommon to witness suicidal behavior as well as substance abuse in connection with the condition. In rare cases, the degree of the fear of having the disease can be very strong, approaching a delusional proportion.

Often, the patient's social and family life is seriously affected by the constant preoccupation, fears, and ongoing medical investigations. In mild cases, functioning at work may not be affected, but in severe hypochondriasis, the preoccupation may interfere with job performance and attendance.

Hypochondriasis is believed to be strongly related to Somatization Disorder. In fact, some authors believe that the two conditions are merely different manifestations of the same phenomenon. Furthermore, it has been reported that about one third of patients with functional somatic symptoms have at least transient hypochondriacal concerns (Kellner, 1991).

Case Example

Mark was 43 years old and had been a school teacher for over 10 years. His wife described him as "always uptight." "He was never able to relax to enjoy anything," she added. He had come to the psychiatrist reluctantly; his neurologist had told him that he would not see him anymore, and his wife forced him to come. He was visibly anxious and looked serious, "I think I have a brain tumor, but everybody tells me I am just imagining it. Is it possible that the brain scan did not pick it up? I heard that the MRI would be more reliable, but Dr. Smith refused to order it. Can you order it for me?" Mark proceeded to describe his symptoms, which sounded like a textbook case of a brain tumor: "I am dizzy, I have double vision, I can't keep my balance, my left leg is weak, I wake up with severe headache every morning...so what can be causing all of that?" Detailed history of the patient revealed that he was always afraid that he might get a serious disease. He was interested in medical literature and made regular visits to his doctor and always asked for a thorough examination. His wife added that a few weeks before he got "sick," his uncle had died from a stroke, and soon after that, she lost her job and he became very worried about money.

Over the following weeks, the patient's fear of having a brain tumor and his "physical" complaints waxed and waned as he attended weekly psychotherapy sessions and took an antidepressant medication. Although he continued to request medical examinations and tests, he was discouraged gently but firmly, and was constantly reassured that he was in good physical health. He was able to talk about his other worries, about his anger toward his boss, and about his fear of failure. As the treatment progressed, the patient showed gradual improvement. After a few months of therapy, the frequency of sessions was reduced, and he was seen monthly for medication management and support. Although most of his fears dissipated, and he was able to function well at work and at home, he still harbored the "hidden" fear that he still might have a brain tumor. On his last visit he said smirking, "You made me have some doubts about my condition, but I still get the fear and the symptoms from time to time. I guess I have to live with that."

The fact that this patient did not recover completely is typical and reflects the difficult nature and the chronic course of hypochondriasis. However, proper interventions can certainly improve the quality of the patient's life.

ETIOLOGY AND CONTRIBUTING FACTORS

The classic psychoanalytic explanation of hypochondriasis, as in other Somatoform Disorders, views the physical aspects of the syndrome as the unconsciously chosen means by which the patient expresses underlying psychological conflict so that the potential anxiety that might arise from bringing the conflict to the conscious level can be avoided. Other psychological theories have attempted to explain the origin of hypochondriasis in different ways, including disturbed object relations, repressed hostility, masochism, guilt, conflicted dependency needs, defense against feelings of low self-esteem and inadequacy, perceptual and cognitive abnormalities, and reinforcement for playing the "sick role" (Martin & Yutzy, 1994).

At particular risk for developing hypochondriasis are people with a history of serious medical illnesses in childhood. It can also be precipitated by the death or serious illness of a close friend or a family member.

Some researchers believe that other psychiatric disorders, including major depression and Generalized Anxiety Disorder, could be responsible, at least in part, for the condition.

DIAGNOSIS AND DIFFERENTIAL DIAGNOSIS

Patients with hypochondriasis tend to go into meticulous and lengthy detail about their condition. Like patients with other Somatoform Disorders, they go from one doctor to another in search of answers, and they fiercely resist the idea of seeing a psychiatrist.

Hypochondriasis must be differentiated from actual physical illness by performing appropriate physical examinations and diagnostic investigations. It is important to keep in mind that patients with a history of hypochondriasis may also suffer from actual physical illness; unfortunately, it can be overlooked when there is an assumption that the symptoms are not genuine. Proper medical judgment is essential in this regard to pursue appropriate leads and ignore others. Certain serious medical illnesses—such as multiple sclerosis, myasthenia gravis, systemic lupus erythematosus, occult malignancies, and endocrine disorders (DSM-IV, 1994)—present with atypical and inconsistent features that may suggest to the physician the presence of a Somatoform Disorder. Therefore, it is important to keep an open mind when dealing with patients with vague and multiple complaints.

Hypochondriasis needs to be differentiated from major depression, Anxiety Disorder, Obsessive-Compulsive Disorder, Delusional Disorder (somatic type), schizophrenia, Somatization Disorder, Body Dysmorphic Disorder, Factitious Disorder with physical symptoms, and malingering. In major depression, the fear of physical illness and somatic preoccupation can be severe. In such cases, the presence of other symptoms of depression and the relatively quick remission of the somatic complaints as the depression is brought under control can be of help in making the differential diagnosis.

In Anxiety and Panic Disorders, physical complaints and fear of such symptoms can be similar to those in cases of hypochondriasis. Quick remission in response to anxiolytic agents is often adequate to rule out hypochondriasis.

In Obsessive-Compulsive Disorder, some patients develop intrusive thoughts related to fear of disease. Other features of the disorder are usually present and often facilitate the differential diagnosis.

In Delusional Disorder, somatic type, and schizophrenia, patients can present with somatic delusions that may resemble hypochondriasis. It is very rare for the convictions of hypochondriacal patients to reach delusional proportions. History, level of functioning, and the balance of the clinical presentation are often diagnostic of one condition or another.

In Body Dysmorphic Disorder, the preoccupation and ensuing distress usually are centered on the physical appearance of a specific area of the body. In Factitious Disorder, the patient is often seeking the sick role for primary and secondary gains. In malingering, the complaints are usually inconsistent and the patient is often driven by a secondary-gain motive.

TREATMENT APPROACHES

Treatment principles are similar to those followed in the treatment of Somatization Disorder. The therapist must allow the patient to talk about the "physical" problem freely, and must acknowledge the fear and distress endured by the patient. Areas of psychological conflict or stress should be identified and addressed in a subtle way. According to Kellner (1989), it is critical to the progress of therapy that the therapist devise ways to convince the hypochondriacal patient that his or her symptoms are innocuous and that his or her beliefs are false. Such a task may prove difficult since most patients are unwilling to give up their beliefs, and premature confrontation may jeopardize the therapeutic alliance.

Several therapeutic techniques may need to be combined in order for the treatment of hypochondriacal patients to be successful. It is important to explain to the patient, using simple language, the way various symptoms develop on the basis of accurate medical facts. Many patients will understand and even agree, for example, that emotional factors through their effects on the autoimmune system, the endocrine system, and various brain functions are capable of producing a wide variety of somatic symptoms. Such openings allow the therapist to undermine the patient's false convictions and to create adequate doubt in his or her mind in preparation for psychological interpretations. It is useful to repeat explanations and interpretations over time in order to strengthen their impressions. Empathy and support represent the cornerstone of the treatment process; however, other techniques, such as cognitive therapy, suggestion, behavioral therapy, insight-oriented psychotherapy, and group therapy may be employed, depending on the circumstances. Some patients have shown progress in response to physical exercise (Kellner, 1989).

The therapist must maintain close contact with treating

physicians in order to ensure that physical examinations and diagnostic investigations are limited to that which is absolutely necessary to keep the patient reassured and to pursue leads that are likely to be genuinely physical. In chronic cases of hypochondriasis, periodic physical examinations and limited diagnostic procedures may be beneficial for both patient and the therapeutic alliance.

Antidepressant medications and anxiolytics have been reported to be effective in some cases, especially when symptoms of depression or anxiety are of a significant degree. Drug therapy should be maintained for several weeks or months even after the target symptoms have disappeared in order to assure adequate treatment and to minimize chances of recurrence. In treatment-resistant patients, electroconvulsive therapy (ECT) may be needed, especially in those with major depression (Kellner, 1989).

COURSE AND PROGNOSIS

Hypochondriasis tends to take a chronic course, going through cycles of exacerbation and remission. In some cases, complete recovery can occur. Social, occupational, and other important areas of functioning are likely to suffer a great deal as a result of the illness. Acute onset, the presence of a true medical condition, the absence of a Personality Disorder, and the absence of secondary gain are favorable prognostic indicators (DSM-IV, 1994).

It is estimated that about one quarter of patients with the full syndrome of hypochondriasis do poorly, two thirds undergo a chronic course with a fluctuation of symptoms, and one tenth of patients recover. The course of mild hypochondriasis varies considerably among patients (Martin & Yutzy, 1994).

4

BODY DYSMORPHIC DISORDER

DEFINITION AND CLINICAL FEATURES

Body Dysmorphic Disorder (dysmorphophobia) refers to the preoccupation with a defect in appearance based on a false conviction that a certain part of the body is ugly or deformed. The defect is either imagined entirely, or is minor, but exaggerated by the patient (DSM-IV, 1994). The preoccupation often causes significant distress or impairment in important aspects of the person's life, including social and occupational areas. Reassurances by medical personnel or others usually do not lead to any relief.

Areas that commonly become the focus of the patient's preoccupation include the face and head. Thinning hair, acne, facial asymmetry, or the shape or size of the nose, ears, eyes, or mouth are among the usual complaints. Preoccupation with the breasts, buttocks, abdomen, genitals, or legs is also found.

The disorder is encountered among young men and women equally, and it often begins during adolescence. De Leon, Bott, and Simpson (1989) report that it also frequently occurs among women at menopause.

ASSOCIATED FEATURES

Patients tend to avoid discussing any details concerning their "defect" with others due to embarrassment and discomfort. They often feel devastated, pained, and angered by the perceived defect, which they believe to have destroyed their lives. Consequently, they spend their time thinking about the "defect," checking the mirror, grooming, and examining themselves. Some patients attempt to camouflage the "defect," growing a beard to cover imagined facial scars, wearing a hat to hide imagined hair loss, or stuffing the shorts to enhance a "small" penis (DSM-IV, 1994).

The degree to which the patient believes in his or her imagined defect may reach a delusional proportion. Some patients experience paranoid thinking and feel that others are talking about their deformity. These individuals are often self-conscious and tend to avoid social settings, shy away from close relationships, and become isolated. Some may drop out of school or leave their jobs and may become housebound for years. The disorder can cause marital problems and even divorce.

The degree of preoccupation with the imagined defect and the behavior that follows resemble symptoms encountered in Obsessive-Compulsive Disorder. Depression or anxiety symptoms may develop in chronic cases. Suicidal ideation and suicide attempts, as well as completed suicides, have been reported.

Patients may pursue various medical, dental, or surgical treatments in order to improve their appearance. Such treatments can lead to serious complications and, in fact, cause the appearance to worsen, which in turn will lead to greater preoccupation and distress. It is rare for patients with Body Dysmorphic Disorder to seek psychiatric help on their own. Most patients seen in psychiatric settings are referred by specialists, such as plastic surgeons, dermatologists, and otolaryngologists (De Leon, et al., 1989).

Body Dysmorphic Disorder may be associated with other psychiatric disorders, including major depression, Delusional Disorder, social phobia, and Obsessive-Compulsive Disorder (DSM-IV, 1994).

Case Example

Todd was a 22-year-old college student who came to the office complaining: "My nose is too big. It is very embarrassing to be with people." Todd was neatly dressed and was somewhat shy. He spoke in a soft voice and had poor eye contact with the psychiatrist. "I don't think that you have a big nose," the psychiatrist replied in a confident voice. "That's what everyone says, but I think they are just trying to make me to feel better," the patient responded.

Todd told the psychiatrist that he had been turned down by so many girls because of his nose that he had given up on women. "I tried to get my nose fixed, but the plastic surgeon did not think that she could do much for me," he said. The psychiatrist listened to Todd and then asked: "So what do you think that I can do for you?" "I am not sure; my parents want me to talk to somebody. They think it is all in my head," he replied.

Further history revealed that Todd lacked confidence in many areas of his life. He was dependent on his mother for almost everything. He described her as strong and controlling. He described his father as cold and demanding. He missed many days from school because he felt that other students made fun of him because of his "ugly" nose. He had no friends and spent most of his time at home, mostly thinking about his nose and all the misery it had caused him.

Treatment was difficult and frustrating. Todd was very resistant to psychotherapy and argued with every interpretation that was made by the psychiatrist. He showed minor response to the antipsychotic drug pimozide, but he discontinued treatment few weeks later, and no further follow-up was available.

ETIOLOGY AND CONTRIBUTING FACTORS

There is considerable argument among researchers and clinicians in reference to whether Body Dysmorphic Disorder constitutes a discrete entity or is simply a subtype of another disorder. It has been suggested that the disorder may represent a variant of social phobia, Obsessive-Compulsive Disorder, depression, hypochondriasis, or Delusional Disorder. The *International Statistical Classification of Diseases and Related Health Problems* (ICD-10) classifies it as a subtype of hypochondriasis (Martin & Yutzy, 1994).

No specific causes have been identified in connection with this disorder. As indicated, Body Dysmorphic Disorder may be considered a subtype of other psychiatric disorders, and hence it may be caused by factors similar to those responsible for such disorders.

DIAGNOSIS AND DIFFERENTIAL DIAGNOSIS

The diagnosis of Body Dysmorphic Disorder is rather straightforward based on the absence of physical evidence in support of the given claim. The disorder needs to be differentiated from normal concerns about appearance where the degree of preoccupation is minimal and does not affect social or occupational functioning. The condition may resemble somatic delusions seen in schizophrenia; however, the absence of other psychotic symptoms can help in the differential diagnosis. Delusional Disorder, somatic type, needs to be differentiated from Body Dysmorphic Disorder. In Delusional Disorder, somatic type, the delusion is often bizarre. However, when the intensity of Body Dysmorphic Disorder reaches a delusional proportion, the diagnosis of Delusional Disorder, somatic type, may also be given. The disorder needs to be differentiated, as well, from cases of major depression where the preoccupation is usually limited to mood-congruent ruminations involving appearance that occur exclusively during the depressive episode. Patients with Obsessive-Compulsive Disorder may become obsessed with certain aspects of their appearance and may exhibit compulsive behavior in that regard. In addition, similar preoccupation and behavior may be seen in the course of social phobia or Avoidant Personality Disorder.

The diagnosis of Body Dysmorphic Disorder should not be made if the symptoms can be fully accounted for by another mental disorder, such as major depression or Delusional Disorder. Furthermore, the diagnosis does not apply to the excessive preoccupation with fatness or body shape secondary to anorexia nervosa. It also does not apply to the discomfort and preoccupation with sex characteristics in cases of Gender Identity Disorder.

Koro refers to the preoccupation that the penis is shrinking and may disappear into the abdomen, resulting in the death of the individual. The condition is considered to be culture-bound and occurs primarily in Southeast Asia. Koro may be related to Body Dysmorphic Disorder, yet it is different in that it is usually brief, associated with severe anxiety and fear of death, responds to positive reassurances, and could occur as an epidemic in certain cultures. Most patients are often troubled by what they consider excessive sexual behavior and fear about their virility. It has been suggested that Koro may result from the interaction of cultural, social, and psychodynamic factors in predisposed individuals. It has also been considered a form of depersonalization syndrome affecting the integrity of the body image (Yap, 1965).

TREATMENT APPROACHES

Treatment is usually difficult owing to the patient's reluctance to explore psychological issues or to question his or her own beliefs. The principles of therapy are similar to those followed in patients with hypochondriasis. A combination of supportive, behavioral, cognitive, and insight-oriented therapies may be helpful.

Antipsychotic drugs, including pimozide (an agent described as effective in monodelusional syndromes), have not shown any significant effectiveness in ameliorating the symptoms of Body Dysmorphic Disorder. Antidepressants, such as clomipramine (Anafranil), and the new selective serotonin reuptake inhibitors (Prozac, Zoloft, and Paxil) have been reported to be fairly effective in the treatment of the disorder. Phillips, McElroy, Keck, et al. (1993) reported that over 50 percent of patients in their study showed a partial or complete remission after being treated with either clomipramine (Anafranil) or fluoxetine (Prozac) regardless of the presence of a major depression or Obsessive-Compulsive Disorder. Anxiolytic agents may be effective, as well. Lexotanil (bromazepam), a benzodiazepine that is not available in the United States, was reported to be effective in a case of Body Dysmorphic Disorder (Martin & Yutzy, 1994).

COURSE AND PROGNOSIS

The onset may be sudden or gradual. The course is chronic and persistent with few symptom-free intervals. In certain patients, the same preoccupation remains unchanged, whereas in others, the original symptoms may disappear, only to be replaced by a new set of concerns and preoccupations (Phillips et al., 1993).

The prognosis is generally not favorable. Many complications can develop in severe cases, including depression, social isolation, marital problems, medical and surgical complications, and suicide.

5

PAIN DISORDER

DEFINITION AND CLINICAL PRESENTATIONS

Pain is one of the most common and significant symptoms encountered in the field of medicine. It serves as a protective mechanism for the purpose of alerting the patient to the presence of a disease or injury, which then makes it feasible to identify and treat the underlying disease. A good example is chest pain in the course of a heart attack or abdominal pain in the case of appendicitis.

It is extremely difficult to define pain because of its subjective quality and the emotional factors often involved. However, the Subcommittee on Taxonomy of the International Association for the Study of Pain defines pain as "an unpleasant sensory and emotional experience associated with actual or potential tissue damage, or described in terms of such damage" (Merskey, 1986). The Committee on Pain, Disability, and Chronic Illness Behavior appointed by the Institute of Medicine elaborated that "the experience of pain is more than a simple sensory process. It is a complex perception involving higher levels of the central nervous system, emotional states, and higher order mental process" (Osterweis, Kleinman, & Mechanic, 1987).

Pain may be experienced by the individual as a single symptom, as in trigeminal neuralgia, or it may occur as

33

part of a complicated condition where other symptoms and signs are present, as in the case of pancreatitis. DSM-IV (1994) outlines the diagnostic criteria of Pain Disorder as pain of sufficient severity that occurs in one or more anatomical sites and that warrants clinical attention. The pain causes significant distress or impairment in social and occupational areas. In addition, the DSM-IV indicates that the disorder may be triggered, exacerbated, or maintained by psychological factors. It also requires that the pain is not intentionally produced or feigned, as in malingering or Factitious Disorder; that it is not better accounted for by Mood Disorder, anxiety, or psychosis; and that it does not meet the criteria for dyspareunia (painful intercourse).

It is important to emphasize that while pain may be heavily influenced by psychological factors, and there may not be adequate physical evidence to account for the severity of pain, patients with Pain Disorder actually feel the pain as they describe it and are sincere in their complaints. This important point distinguishes such patients from others with Factitious Disorders and from malingerers.

SUBTYPES

Although for the most part pain is considered a symptom of general medical conditions, it is fairly common to encounter Pain Disorders that are mainly caused by psychological factors, or at least where such factors seem to exaggerate minor pains that are caused by actual medical conditions. DSM-IV (1994) proposes three subtypes:

Pain Disorder Associated with Psychological Factors

Pain Disorder Associated with Both Psychological Factors and a General Medical Condition

Pain Disorder Associated with a General Medical Condition

The last subtype is not considered a mental disorder and is coded on Axis III. The role of psychological factors in this subtype is minimal or absent.

If the duration of pain is less than six months, the disorder is specified as acute, whereas if the duration is more than six months, the disorder is specified as chronic (DSM-IV, 1994).

ASSOCIATED FEATURES

Pain Disorder often leads to serious disruption in the patient's occupational and social life. Repeated absences from work, disabilities, and unemployment are frequent consequences among patients with chronic Pain Disorders. Serious marital and family problems are also common. Patients typically seek medical attention regularly, and often use or abuse various painkillers. Anger, anxiety, insomnia, depression, and suicidal behavior are usual in the course of chronic pain.

It appears that the prevalence of pain among individuals with psychiatric disorders is higher than that in the general population. Certain studies have shown that pain was much more frequent among patients with "neurotic" disorders than among those with Psychotic Disorders. Chronic pain is most common among patients with major depression, dysthymia, and Adjustment Disorder with depressed mood. In addition, certain forms of acute pain have been reported in patients with Panic Disorder (King & Strain, 1994).

Case Example

Ruth was a 43-year-old woman who had worked as a home health aide for seven years before she sustained a low back injury while trying to lift a patient. She experienced severe back pain that radiated to both legs. The pain interfered with her ability to function, as her job required a certain amount of lifting and driving. The patient was placed on workers' compensation disability while medical treatment proceeded. Physical examinations showed muscular spasm and tenderness over certain areas. Radiological investigations and MRI of the spine did not show any evidence of herniated disks, fractures, or any abnormalities that might account for the reported pain and its distribution. The patient was treated with physical therapy, muscle relaxants, and several combinations of painkillers and anti-inflammatory agents. The patient showed minimal response and was still unable to return to work four months after the onset of her injury. She was referred to the psychiatrist when her treating physician insisted that her condition was not improving sufficiently, based on the clinical findings, and suggested that her emotional condition could be interfering with her recovery.

The patient came to the office willingly and was pleasant and cooperative. She appeared sincere in her description of her symptoms, and her work record showed excellent performance and no evidence of prior illness or absenteeism. Clinical evaluation revealed a history of depression of moderate severity following the accident. In addition, she was experiencing serious conflict in her marriage as her husband was threatening to leave because of problems with her children from a previous marriage. The patient was treated with an antidepressant medication and was seen weekly for psychotherapy that helped her express her anger and fear and encouraged her to return to work. Within three months, the patient was able to work on a part-time basis, and a few weeks later she resumed her regular job and schedule. Antidepressant medication and psychotherapy were continued for several months after she returned to work. The patient experienced recurrent episodes of back pain from time to time, but she was able to cope with it and to maintain her employment.

ETIOLOGY AND CONTRIBUTING FACTORS

Although pain has not traditionally been considered a mental disorder and is often caused by an underlying general medical condition, most clinicians and researchers agree that psychological and social factors play an important role especially in chronic conditions. Several investigators have studied various ethnic and religious groups comparing pain tolerance and attitude toward pain. The studies suggest that there are significant cultural differences with regard to pain tolerance and expression of pain (Chapman & Turner, 1990). A certain injury may cause a significant amount of pain in one individual, for example, yet it may cause little or no pain in another. Furthermore, the perception of pain by the same individual may vary from one social setting to another. Pre-existing personality organization and prior experiences are most important in this respect. Unconscious conflicts, dependency issues, attention seeking, and secondary gain are also very important factors. It is most likely that the perception of pain that is experienced by an individual is determined by a dynamic interaction among physical, psychological, and social factors.

Pain may occur at any age, and it tends to occur more frequently in females than in males. It has been shown that first-degree relatives of patients with chronic Pain Disorder are more likely to show evidence of Depressive Disorders, alcohol dependence, and chronic pain, thus, suggesting a genetic factor.

DIAGNOSIS AND DIFFERENTIAL DIAGNOSIS

It is essential that thorough physical examinations and appropriate diagnostic investigations be performed in all cases of Pain Disorder in order to identify any general medical condition that may be responsible for the pain. It is also important to assess the degree of reported pain in relation to the actual medical condition in order to identify the presence of psychological factors that may be responsible for the exacerbation or persistence of pain.

Pain Disorder needs to be differentiated from Somatization Disorder, where the complaints are numerous and pain is only one aspect of the condition. In Conversion Disorder, the symptoms are not limited to pain by definition. Pain in the course of Factitious Disorder is usually feigned in order to assume the sick role; in malingering, the pain is produced intentionally for the purpose of secondary gain.

PAIN MANAGEMENT

Prior to the initiation of any serious pain management program, it is essential to conduct a comprehensive assessment of the clinical presentation in order to evaluate the underlying medical condition, the psychological factors, and the social or environmental factors that may be contributing to the condition. Treatment of Pain Disorder may include some or all of the following treatment modalities.

Painkillers

Painkillers include opioid analgesics and nonsteroidal anti-inflammatory agents. It is always advised to avoid the use of opioid analgesics unless they are absolutely essential, for obvious reasons related to potential abuse and dependency. Such problems can complicate the clinical picture and add more difficulties for the already troubled patient. Opioid analgesics may be used more liberally in patients with terminal illness to provide them with an adequate level of comfort.

Psychotropic Agents

In addition to their antidepressant effect, certain tricyclic antidepressants, such as amitriptyline and nortriptyline, in small doses, have been shown to be effective in alleviating chronic pain. Antidepressant medications, including the new selective serotonin reuptake inhibitors, may need to be used for the treatment of depressive symptoms that have preceded or followed Pain Disorder. Benzodiazepines have also been useful in patients with pain, especially when anxiety is complicating the clinical picture. However, the physician must keep in mind the potential for addiction and dependency, especially in chronic pain cases. Lithium, Tegretol, Depakote, and certain neuroleptics have also been shown to be effective in the management of chronic pain (King & Strain, 1994).

Psychotherapies

Individual psychotherapy may be helpful in cases where psychological conflicts seem to be influencing the degree or the duration of Pain Disorder. Supportive, behavioral, cognitive, and insight-oriented techniques can be combined as needed based on the clinical situation. Group therapy may be helpful to some individuals; for example, self-help groups, such as fibromyalgia and endometriosis support groups, are particularly effective. Marital counseling and family therapy may be needed in cases where marital problems and other family issues arise as a result of chronic pain.

Relaxation and Biofeedback

Relaxation and biofeedback techniques can be very beneficial in cases where simple pain management has not been successful. Such methods can be used alone or in conjunction with other treatment modalities. Relaxation can reduce emotional tension, which often exaggerates the perception of painful stimuli. Biofeedback also provides ways of lowering emotional stress and distracting the patient from his or her preoccupation with pain.

Hypnosis

Hypnosis and posthypnotic suggestions may be helpful in highly amenable individuals. Such methods have been shown through controlled studies to be effective in patients with disseminated breast cancer and low back pain. Hypnosis is seldom effective if used alone, but rather must be combined with other modalities (Blackwell, Merskey, & Kellner, 1989).

Sensory Stimulation

In cases of chronic pain, *transcutaneous electrical nerve stimulation* (TENS) may be employed. The theory behind this method is that the alteration of sensory input may block or alleviate the pain centrally through the release of endorphin and serotonin.

Acupuncture is another well-known technique to treat pain utilizing the same sensory stimulation principle as TENS.

Nerve Block

A widely used method for chronic and intractable pain, the technique consists of injecting local anesthetics into the epidural space. This method may be helpful to patients with chronic low back pain. *Trigger point injection* is another technique that may be used in the management of chronic pain.

Surgical Procedures

In some cases, where other treatments prove unsuccessful, invasive surgical procedures may be inevitable. These include spinal cord stimulation, brain implantation of electrodes, and leukotomy.

Other Treatments

Electroconvulsive therapy (ECT) has been used with controversial efficacy in some patients with intractable pain. Low-power laser irradiation and intravenous administration of a delta sleep-inducing neuropeptide (DSLP), two experimental techniques, have shown encouraging results in the management of chronic pain (Blackwell et al., 1989).

Rehabilitation

Physical therapy may offer a considerable amount of relief to certain patients with chronic Pain Disorder. Rehabilitation that may involve both physical as well as social aspects should be considered in all chronic cases where complete recovery is deemed unlikely. Changes in occupation, living arrangement, and social relations may be inevitable. Support groups, behavior modification, and psychotherapy may prove to be invaluable in such instances.

The treatment goals of Pain Disorder should focus on the alleviation of pain as much as possible and on improving the patient's coping mechanisms and general functioning. Whereas it may be feasible to achieve such goals in cases of acute pain, the situation is much more difficult in chronic Pain Disorder. In such instances, it is important to address the psychological problems and the social factors that may be interfering with patient's progress.

COURSE AND PROGNOSIS

Acute pain may resolve within hours or days; however, when pain does not resolve within a short time, it may become chronic and can lead to occupational and social complications as indicated.

The prognosis of Pain Disorder depends on the under-lying factors. Pain that is caused primarily by medical conditions may resolve or persist depending on the nature and success of the treatment of that condition. Pain that is believed to be primarily caused by psychological factors is more resistant to treatment and may resolve only if the underlying psychological factors can be identified and resolved.

In cases of chronic pain resulting from such injuries as car accidents and work-related injuries, the prognosis can be influenced by issues of litigation and the prospects of secondary gain and financial compensation. The role of the psychiatrist and other mental health professionals becomes more important in such cases.

Part II

*Factitious Disorders
and Malingering*

6

FACTITIOUS DISORDER WITH PHYSICAL SIGNS AND SYMPTOMS

DEFINITION AND CLINICAL PRESENTATION

Factitious Disorder with physical signs and symptoms may be defined as a mental disorder leading the patient to feign multiple physical signs and symptoms for the purpose of assuming the sick role. A chronic and severe variant of this disorder is commonly known as Munchausen's syndrome. Although the disorder is under the voluntary control of the patient, he or she is usually unconscious of the reason for the behavior and does not have a secondary gain. Rather, the behavior is driven by the primary gain, which consists solely of assuming the sick role for a variety of unconscious reasons.

The disorder is particularly common among health care professionals who have some knowledge of physical disease and who may have access to drugs or other medical equipment.

Patients usually go from doctor to doctor and manage to get themselves admitted to different hospitals where they may undergo invasive diagnostic procedures and multiple surgeries. They often create the symptoms by inflicting wounds, ingesting harmful material, causing infections, or simply present with a textbook picture of a serious condition, such as a heart attack or appendicitis. Common clinical presentations include abdominal pain, dizziness, blacking out, hemorrhages, abscesses, and fever of unknown origin.

Even after treatment is initiated, various complications, often induced by the patient, develop unexpectedly and without clear explanation. Ironically, serious complications that can be life threatening do not deter the patient from continuing to play the sick role. Many patients die or are left with serious disabilities. Addiction to painkillers and tranquilizers is common, and this in itself may perpetuate the behavior and motivate the patient to persist in seeking more and more medical treatments and medications.

ASSOCIATED FEATURES

Patients are known to "doctor shop" and to go from one hospital to another, sometimes traveling to different towns where they convince unsuspecting emergency room doctors of their need for hospitalization. Some patients assume different names when admitted in order to avoid being detected through medical records. Patients present their history with dramatic flare and are often inconsistent and vague when questioned in detail. Many patients have extensive knowledge of medical terminology and hospital routines, which they gather from their repeated contacts with doctors and hospitals. Most patients show little affect and inadequate concern in relation to their illness and may exhibit the "la belle indifference" sign often present in patients with Conversion Disorder.

Serious interruptions in occupational, social, and family life are common. In addition, serious medical complications and drug addictions are very common as a result of extensive and often unnecessary interventions.

Case Example

Sarah was an attractive 27-year-old woman who was staying on the surgical service following the amputation of her right leg. The patient had been admitted to the hospital a month earlier after sustaining a compound fracture of the right leg in a motorcycle accident. At that time, the fracture was treated surgically with pins and plates, and the wounds were sutured and dressed. A course of intravenous antibiotics was also initiated to minimize the chance of infection. Shortly after the surgery, the patient spiked a high fever, and the leg became seriously infected. Various treatment strategies were applied unsuccessfully, and the infection continued to worsen. On one occasion, while the surgeon was attempting to debride the wound, he suspected the presence of fecal material in the wound, which proved to be the case upon laboratory testing. The patient was asked about the fecal material but denied any knowledge of it. On another occasion, small pieces of glass were found inside the wound. At this point, it became essential to confront the patient with the fact that she was attempting to cause more damage to her leg and prolong her illness. The patient continued to persist in her denial and became angry with the doctors and nurses. The decision to amputate the leg was made because of serious bone infection and gangrene. When told of that situation, the patient showed little concern about losing her leg and consented to the amputation freely.

When the patient was interviewed by the psychiatrist, she broke down into tears, admitting that the motorcycle accident was somewhat intentional: "But I did not think that it was going to get that bad. They would not admit me to any hospital in New York, they all know me and think I am not really sick. I thought an accident would get me in for sure, then one thing led to another, and here I am without a leg. I did not want to lose my leg, you've got to believe me." She showed genuine emotion. Sarah later spoke of her painful childhood when she was abandoned

48 Psychosomatic Disorders

by her father after her mother died, and she went from one foster home to another. She was always afraid of being abandoned by people whom she loved. She had not at any time in her life been able to have a meaningful relationship with anyone.

Sarah left the hospital with one leg. "Maybe now someone will really care about me," she said with tears in her eyes as she waved goodbye to the doctors and nurses on the floor.

ETIOLOGY AND CONTRIBUTING FACTORS

Most writers and clinicians agree that the main underlying dynamic in cases of Factitious Disorders is the need to play the sick role in order to get attention, support, and sympathy, and to be cared for by others (Folks & Freeman, 1985). As indicated earlier, there is usually no secondary gain here. The behavior seems to fulfill the primary gain of being loved and attended to by a parent figure. It is possible that masochistic and unconscious self-destructive impulses may be involved as well.

Most published case studies suggest that patients with Factitious Disorders had suffered significant emotional and physical deprivation, including parental physical abuse. Common features among such patients include a strong yearning for dependency, masochistic traits, anger over past deprivation, and the need to achieve control and mastery (Eisendrath, 1989).

It has been suggested that possible predisposing factors to Factitious Disorder include the presence of other mental disorders and medical illness during childhood or adolescence that may have led to extensive medical interventions. Other factors include a severe Personality Disorder, such as Borderline Personality Disorder; an important relationship with a physician in the past; a grudge against the medical profession; and being employed in the health care field (DSM-IV, 1994).

DIAGNOSIS AND DIFFERENTIAL DIAGNOSIS

It is important to differentiate Factitious Disorder from true medical conditions by providing appropriate physical examination and reasonable diagnostic procedures. The clinician needs to focus on such objective factors as demographics, family history, associated features, physical findings, treatment response, and long-term outcome (Pope, Jonas, & Jones, 1982).

The diagnosis is usually made when the medical presentation cannot be explained on the basis of medical facts and expected outcome of treatment. Often, laboratory tests yield bizarre and inconsistent results. Unexpected complications and prolonged course of relatively simple diseases may raise the index of suspicion. The fact that a patient seeks treatment repeatedly from different doctors and facilities should alert the clinician to the possibility of Factitious Disorder. Other warning signs include symptoms exhibited only when patients are being observed, pathological lying (pseudologia fantastica), disruptive behavior while hospitalized, unusually extensive knowledge of medical terminology, and evidence of multiple surgeries and medical interventions (DSM-IV, 1994).

Factitious Disorder with physical signs and symptoms should be differentiated from Conversion Disorder, Somatization Disorder, and malingering. In Conversion Disorder, the patient rarely allows invasive procedures or inflicts any serious injuries upon himself or herself. In Somatization Disorder, the complaints are multiple, genuine emotion is shown, and the patient does not cause self-injuries. In malingering, secondary gain is always present, and the patient avoids serious diagnostic procedures or treatments.

Psychological and neuropsychological tests performed on Munchausen patients revealed higher verbal scores than performance scores, deficits in conceptual organizational skills and judgment, and immature, impulsive, histrionic, and narcissistic traits. Patients tended to be passive, had poor body image and sexual identity, and were preoccupied with death, morbid thoughts, depression, and suicidal ideation (Plewes & Fagan, 1994).

TREATMENT APPROACHES

After the patient is identified by the medical team as presenting with a Factitious Disorder, the psychiatrist is often consulted to help in confronting the patient and managing the consequences of the confrontation. It is always preferred that both the psychiatrist and the treating physician approach the patient together. Some professionals recommend against premature confrontation and prefer to wait until the psychiatrist establishes a strong therapeutic relationship with the patient. It is important to present the situation to the patient gently and to emphasize that his or her behavior is driven by serious psychological problems that need to be dealt with. Most patients deny the charges angrily and sign out against medical advice. Those who cooperate with the staff need to be referred to a mental health professional for appropriate intervention (Eisendrath, 1989).

Psychotherapy is the only treatment that is likely to help. Supportive, insight-oriented, and behavioral techniques have been described as effective in some cases. The focus of the treatment should be on the unconscious issues behind the behavior. The therapist must concentrate on the symptoms, the suffering, the anger, and the need to be cared for. Later, the treatment needs to center on helping the patient find alternative behaviors to get attention and affection from others. This involves attempting to enhance the patient's self-esteem, improve his or her interpersonal relationships, and enrich his or her social life in general.

The use of antidepressant medications has been reported to be beneficial in certain cases of Factitious Disorder with physical signs and symptoms (Stone, 1977; Ford,

1983). Van Putten and Alban (1977) reported significant response to lithium therapy in a patient with both Factitious Disorder and Conversion Disorder. The use of other psychotropic medications may be indicated in certain patients, depending on the clinical presentation.

COURSE AND PROGNOSIS

The disorder is more common in males than in females. It may be limited to one or more episodes, but is usually chronic and may follow a pattern of successive hospitalizations. The onset generally occurs during early adulthood, and may be precipitated by a legitimate hospitalization because of a medical or mental illness (DSM-IV, 1994). Other factors that seem to precipitate the disorder include severe sexual or marital stress and fear of abandonment (Plewes & Fagan, 1994). The disorder tends to worsen under severe emotional stress. Improvement and subsequent recovery may begin when emotional needs can be fulfilled through normal and mature relationships.

FACTITIOUS DISORDER BY PROXY

Munchausen's syndrome by proxy refers to the situation where one person induces illness in another for the purpose of indirectly satisfying his or her own unconscious needs. In such cases, the diagnosis is given to the person who induces the symptoms in order to assume the sick role through the "victim." Often, it is a mother who causes an injury or illness in her child, and then seeks treatment along the same lines described earlier in the chapter. Mothers who are identified with this disorder may be given another psychiatric diagnosis, such as a Personality Disorder or depression; however, some have been reported to be psychiatrically "normal" (Plewes & Fagan, 1994). It is probably accurate to conclude, also by "proxy", that the psychodynamic factors involved in Factitious Disorder by proxy are similar to those outlined in patients with primary Factitious Disorder.

For example, a mother was observed by the nursing staff, through a one-way mirror, putting a drop of blood into the container of urine that was taken from her child. In another case, a mother was seen rubbing the thermometer with a blanket to increase the temperature reading in order to convince the doctor to prescribe antibiotics for her child.

Psychotherapy is often helpful in such patients. Techniques and guidelines similar to those outlined for patients with primary Factitious Disorders should be followed. Issues of ambivalence and hostility toward the child may need to be dealt with and family therapy may be indicated in some cases.

7

FACTITIOUS DISORDER WITH PSYCHOLOGICAL SIGNS AND SYMPTOMS

DEFINITION AND CLINICAL PRESENTATION

Factitious Disorder with psychological signs and symptoms may be defined as a mental disorder in which the patient feigns psychiatric symptoms for the sole purpose of playing the sick role and receiving attention through treatment. Here, the patient may also visit emergency rooms seeking admission to psychiatric units and go from one mental health professional to another, presenting with symptoms of depression, psychosis, mania, amnesia, disorientation, transient loss of personal identity, and others. Typically, the symptoms are worse when the patient is being observed by the staff. Often, the history is inconsistent, and the patient may not be able to respond to detailed examination appropriately. Usually, the symptoms reported by the patient represent his or her concept of mental illness and may not conform to any specific disorder as it is known to mental health professionals. Patients often consent to serious treatments, such as ECT and the administration of antipsychotic drugs (DSM-IV, 1994).

Factitious Disorder with psychological signs and symptoms is rare and seems to occur more often in men than in women. Details regarding its epidemiology are not well known. Variants of this disorder have been known as Ganser's syndrome and hysterical psychosis (Merskey, 1979).

ASSOCIATED FEATURES

This disorder is often associated with severe Personality Disorders, such as Borderline Personality Disorder and Antisocial Personality Disorder. Occasionally, patients resort to using certain drugs, such as stimulants, tranquilizers, hallucinogens, or a combination of multiple drugs, in order to produce specific symptoms to convince the clinician of their illness. When questioned in detail by clinicians, some patients may respond to simple direct questions by giving approximate answers. For example, the clinician may ask the patient: "How much is four plus four?", and the patient may answer "Seven," thereby giving the impression that there is something wrong with his or her thinking process. The patient is usually alert and shows no evidence of organic impairment.

Complications, including side effects and addiction to psychotropic medications, are common. In addition, deterioration in family, social, and occupational areas often follows chronic Factitious Disorder with psychological signs and symptoms.

It is fairly common for Factitious Disorder with psychological signs and symptoms to be present together with Factitious Disorder with physical signs and symptoms, making management more complicated.

Case Example

Frank was a 38-year-old man who was admitted to the psychiatric unit because of symptoms of depression and suicidal ideation. The patient was interviewed by different staff members on separate occasions during the first two days of his admission. During the morning report, each staff member seemed to have a different version of what had led to Frank's admission. The information appeared to be inconsistent, although all incidents reported were colorful and dramatic. On the ward, the patient was observed by the staff to be very involved with other patients and seemed to be enjoying his stay. He did not show any evidence of appetite or sleep disturbances, which he had reported on admission. The patient refused to allow any staff member to contact his wife; rather he called her repeatedly on the pay telephone. A review of the emergency room record revealed that Frank had been evaluated seven other times during the preceding two years for different psychiatric symptoms, including suicidal gestures, depression, hallucinations, and memory loss.

The patient wanted to be given antidepressant medication and sleeping pills. When told that he did not have enough symptoms to warrant such treatment, he became angry and insisted that he felt depressed and had not slept well the night before. At this point, the staff became highly suspicious of the case and insisted on having a family meeting with his wife if he were to stay on the unit. Frank's wife was very angry with him and told the staff that he had been doing this for three years and that whenever he become stressed out on the job, he wanted to be admitted to the hospital for a while. She felt that the marriage had suffered and that his associates at work were beginning to wonder about his absenteeism.

Frank was confronted by the staff and was told that he had serious psychiatric problems that needed to be dealt with, but that he was not depressed and he did not need to be kept in the hospital. He was referred to outpatient individual therapy, which he continued for several months.

ETIOLOGY AND CONTRIBUTING FACTORS

As indicated earlier, the primary motive for all Factitious Disorders is the need to play the sick role for the purpose of getting attention, sympathy, and support from people who are in the position of authority. Similar to Factitious Disorder with physical signs and symptoms, a history of trauma during childhood including sexual and physical abuse, neglect, and abandonment, may be present. The patient may have been exposed as a child to a close relative who was mentally ill, and that experience, relegated to the unconscious for years, may trigger the onset of a Factitious Disorder.

Severe environmental stress and preexisting Personality Disorders seem to predispose to the onset of this condition.

DIAGNOSIS AND DIFFERENTIAL DIAGNOSIS

There are several clues that can help the clinician identify patients with Factitious Disorders. These include inconsistencies in the history given to different people, the unusual combination and presentation of various symptoms, pathological lying (pseudologia fantastica), a history of multiple visits to various providers and facilities presenting with different stories, and a mental status examination that does not confirm the complaints of the patient.

Obviously, Factitious Disorder with psychological signs and symptoms must be differentiated from true psychiatric disorders, such as schizophrenia, other Psychotic Disorders, and major depression. For this purpose, a careful history, including information obtained from family member, is extremely important. Psychological testing may be helpful in some cases; however, there is no specific test to identify such patients, and the responses are often variable and inconsistent.

The disorder should be differentiated from dementia and other "organic" mental disorders, including drug intoxication, where the presentation may be inconsistent and mixed (Asaad, 1995). It should also be differentiated from malingering, where secondary gain is present. If the patient meets the diagnostic criteria for a Personality Disorder, such diagnosis should be noted on Axis II separately.

TREATMENT APPROACHES

Little has been written about the treatment of Factitious Disorder with psychological symptoms. However, as in Factitious Disorders with physical signs and symptoms, the only appropriate and possibly effective treatment modality is that of individual psychotherapy. The patient must be told that it is not necessary to treat the symptoms that he or she is reporting to the staff and that it is more important to identify and treat the problems that caused him or her to seek the role of a mentally ill person. The patient will be expecting attention, sympathy, and support, all of which should be provided for the purpose of engaging him or her. The contributing factors and the unconscious issues can be identified and interpreted as treatment proceeds. A combination of supportive, cognitive, behavioral, and insight-oriented techniques may be utilized. Treatment is often long term and depends on the degree of patient cooperation.

Antidepressant medication may be helpful in some cases, and other psychotropic medications may be used as clinically indicated.

COURSE AND PROGNOSIS

The disorder may be limited to one or two brief episodes; however, it may become chronic in some cases. Remission can be spontaneous or may occur with successful psychotherapy. When Factitious Disorder with physical signs and symptoms is also present, the prognosis is worse, and treatment becomes more difficult.

8

MALINGERING

DEFINITION AND CLINICAL PRESENTATION

Malingering may be defined as an act of deception in which the individual pretends to be ill for the purpose of attaining a secondary gain. Most often, the patient is trying to avoid work or to obtain certain compensation for being sick. This kind of behavior is most common in prisons and military settings where it is engaged in to secure a transfer into a better environment or to avoid certain responsibilities. It is also common following car accidents or work-related injuries for the purpose of litigation to gain monetary compensation.

Malingering can refer to the total fabrication and invention of symptoms or to the exaggeration of existing minor symptoms. Patients often report unusual symptoms with notable inconsistencies. The symptoms are usually dramatic and colorful. Typically, physical examination and laboratory investigations fail to confirm the reported symptoms, and some patients may confess under pressure to their deceptive behavior.

No demographic data are available regarding malingering. Based on clinical experience, however, it seems to be found more often among males than among females, and tends to occur during early adulthood. The behavior is often limited to specific situations and usually disappears as soon as the secondary gain is attained.

ASSOCIATED FEATURES

Malingering is commonly seen in patients with Antisocial Personality Disorder. It may also be observed in patients with histrionic and dependent traits. In some cases, other psychiatric diagnoses may be identified in connection with malingering, including schizophrenia, depression, Somatization Disorder, and substance abuse.

Case Example

Ted was a 26-year-old single man who reported severe back pain upon lifting a box during a regular day of work at a supermarket warehouse. The patient was sent to a doctor who examined him and did not find any evidence of physical injury. The patient was given a mild pain-killer and sent home on a three-day sick leave to rest. At the end of the sick leave, Ted continued to report pain and told his doctor that the pain was traveling down his legs and that his feet were becoming numb. Neurological examination was requested and failed to confirm the complaints based on anatomical distribution of the nerves. An MRI of the back revealed a normal spine and no evidence of a herniated disk or tissue damage. However, Ted continued to complain of pain and was still staying home from work six weeks after the alleged injury, collecting full pay from workers' compensation. Ted was ordered to undergo a series of special tests at Work-Lab, designed to detect unsuspecting malingerers. He showed glaring inconsistencies that confirmed the suspicions of all the physicians involved. The patient was given the choice of either returning to work or being fired. He chose to return to work. When seen by the psychiatrist, Ted confessed that he was tired of his job and that he needed a break and some money. He was not interested in psychiatric follow-up.

ETIOLOGY AND CONTRIBUTING FACTORS

The essential motive behind all cases of malingering involves secondary gain. Other unconscious psychodynamic factors may be present, as well. As indicated earlier, Antisocial Personality Disorder is considered a strong predisposing factor.

DIAGNOSIS AND DIFFERENTIAL DIAGNOSIS

Malingering can be suspected whenever a strong secondary gain is a possibility. Inconsistencies in the history reported by the patient, along with negative findings based on physical examination and laboratory investigations, often confirm the suspicion and prompt the physician to make the diagnosis and, perhaps, confront the patient. DSM-IV (1994) suggests that any of the following observations should raise the suspicion of malingering: (1) the presence of a medicolegal situation; (2) marked discrepancy between reported symptoms and objective findings; (3) lack of cooperation with evaluation and treatment; and (4) the presence of Antisocial Personality Disorder. If Antisocial Personality Disorder can be documented, it should be noted on Axis II.

Malingering can be very difficult to prove. Various methods have been employed in attempts to detect deception, including the administration of personality inventories, such as MMPI; the use of structured clinical interviews; giving specialized tests designed to discriminate between actual and exaggerated deficits, and interviewing the patient while he or she is under the influence of amobarbital. In certain forensic cases, polygraphic testing in combination with other methods designed to detect deception has been used. Observance of the patient when he or she is not expecting to be observed may require detective rather than clinical work, but this method can prove to be most reliable in sorting out malingerers from real patients (Kellner, 1991).

Malingering should be differentiated from Factitious Disorders where secondary gain is absent. It should also be differentiated from Conversion Disorder and other Somatoform Disorders where secondary gain is absent and the complaints are often driven by psychodynamic factors or unconscious conflicts.

TREATMENT APPROACHES

Most patients with a history of malingering refuse psychiatric interventions. Motivated patients may benefit from individual psychotherapy to provide support and explore the psychological reasons behind the behavior.

COURSE AND PROGNOSIS

In most cases, the behavior is episodic and is limited to the situation where secondary gain is sought. In cases where severe Personality Disorder is present, the behavior may take a chronic course. Confrontation and threats of legal action can be effective in discouraging certain patients from lengthy deceptive behavior.

Part III

*Medical Conditions
Affected by
Psychological Factors*

9

GASTROINTESTINAL DISORDERS AFFECTED BY PSYCHOLOGICAL FACTORS

The relationship between the gut and emotional stress has long been documented by clinicians and researchers. Psychological factors seem to influence various functions of the gastrointestinal system and may play a significant role in the onset, manifestations, and course of several gastrointestinal disorders. Anxiety and panic attacks, for example, can cause difficulty in swallowing, stomach pain, and diarrhea. Depression can lead to appetite changes, constipation, and preoccupation with bowel functions. However, the focus of this chapter will be on the more serious and specific gastrointestinal disorders that seem to be heavily influenced by various psychological factors.

GLOBUS, FEAR OF CHOKING, AND DYSPHAGIA

Clinical Features

Globus or globus hystericus refers to the sensation of a lump in the throat in the absence of any physical cause.

The patient may feel that something is stuck in his or her throat, and the sensation may or may not be relieved by swallowing. Typically, and unlike fear of choking and dysphagia, the condition does not occur during eating. It has been estimated that about 4 percent of referrals to otolaryngologists are diagnosed with functional globus (Clouse, 1992). Furthermore, the condition appears to be more common in women than in men, and most patients who seek help at ENT clinics are between the ages of 41 and 50 years (Kellner, 1991).

Fear of choking or pseudodysphagia refers to the inability to swallow or difficulty in swallowing that is caused by the patient's fear of choking during eating. Typically, the fear is limited to swallowing solid food; however, some patients also may be afraid to drink. Patients are often anxious and may lose weight, as they do not eat adequate amounts of food. The prevalence of this condition is not known.

Dysphagia refers to difficulty in swallowing that may be caused by physical or psychological factors. The patient reports that the food sticks in the upper or middle part of the esophagus. The condition may be associated with pain, regurgitation, and aspiration. Esophageal spasm and other motility disorders may lead to chest pain that can mimic a heart attack.

Etiology and Contributing Psychological Factors

In the absence of any physical cause for globus, several psychological factors have been reported to be responsible for the conditions. Several studies have concluded that patients with globus present with a higher degree of psychopathology as compared with other medical patients. Most professionals view the condition as being similar to Somatization Disorder (Chapter 1), although some consider it a form of a Conversion Disorder (Chapter 2). There is a general consensus, however, that patients with globus do not have histrionic personality traits.

Symptoms of depression, anxiety, and Obsessive-Compulsive Disorder have been reported in such patients (Kellner, 1991).

Fear of choking is often present in conjunction with other psychiatric disorders, such as Panic Disorder and depression. A substantial number of patients date the onset of fear to a specific traumatic event that occurred during eating, such as an episode of actual choking. It is believed that fear during eating, aggravated by dryness in the mouth, can inhibit the swallowing reflex, leading to actual difficulty in swallowing. The repetition of such experiences can create a classic conditioning response, which in turn reinforces the behavior (Kellner, 1991).

Dysphagia can be caused by several physical factors. In many cases where no gross pathology can be found, motility disorder of the esophagus may be responsible for the symptoms. Although no specific psychological factors have been shown to be responsible for esophageal motility disorder, several psychiatric diagnoses have been documented in a large percentage of patients (Clouse, 1992).

Treatment Approaches

Most patients with globus respond well to supportive psychotherapy focusing on explanation and reassurance. Other techniques may be used as well when indicated. In many instances where other psychiatric disorders also exist, successful treatment of such disorders leads to the resolution of globus symptoms. Psychotropic medications may be used when appropriate.

In cases of fear of choking, the most effective treatment modality consists of behavior therapy utilizing desensitization, aversion, and biofeedback (Solyom & Sookman, 1980). Drug therapy with antipanic medications, including tricyclic antidepressants, monoamine oxidase inhibitors, and alprazolam, was reported as effective in several cases (Brown, Schwartz, Summergrad, et al., 1986; Greenberg, Stern, & Weilburg, 1988).

Treatment of dysphagia due to esophageal motility disorder is basically medical or surgical. Psychological treatment also may be helpful, and usually consists of explanation and reassurance. In cases where other psychiatric pathology is identified, appropriate management of accompanying disorders may lead to significant relief of dysphagia. The use of psychotropic medications, particularly trazodone, has also been shown to be effective (Clouse, 1992).

Prognosis

The prognosis of globus is generally good in most patients because patients are not afraid of eating; therefore, they do not lose weight. Gray (1983) conducted a 15-year follow-up study on patients with globus and found that 10 percent of the patients still had their symptoms at that time. Forty-three percent of his sample showed minor recurrences of symptoms during the 15-year period, whereas, another 43 percent had no further symptoms after the initial episode.

Fear of choking, on the other hand, may interfere with eating, leading to serious weight loss. There are no sufficient data on long-term prognosis of this condition. However, patients who were treated with behavior therapy and antipanic drugs showed good response to treatment.

The majority of patients with dysphagia seem to do well with available treatments. Burns, Kellum, Bienvenu, et al. (1985) reported in a 4-year follow-up study that most patients improved, although some continued to experience mild chest pain that did not interfere with daily activities.

PEPTIC ULCER DISEASE AND NONULCER DYSPEPSIAS

Clinical Features

The typical presentation of peptic ulcer is that of epigastric pain when the stomach is empty. The pain is often relieved by food or antacids. The symptoms seem to be aggravated by certain foods and by emotional stress. The disease is twice as common in men as in women and can occur at any age, although the average age of onset is 33 years.

Nonulcer dyspepsias refers to a group of upper gastrointestinal disturbances that are caused by dysfunctions of the gastrointestinal tract that are not related to ulcers. Symptoms include epigastric discomfort or pain, a burning sensation, distension, nausea, and vomiting. The symptoms seem to be aggravated by emotional stress. Gastric symptoms that are not related to peptic ulcers appear to be more common than peptic ulcer, but most complaints are short lived, although the severity of the symptoms and disability can be as great or greater than those related to peptic ulcer (Kellner, 1991).

Etiology and Contributing Psychological Factors

There are several physical factors that seem to contribute to the formation and aggravation of peptic ulcer disease, including hypersecretion of hydrochloric acid; decreased tissue resistance; the use of certain drugs, such as aspirin; smoking; and excessive alcohol intake. Furthermore, genetic inheritance of predisposing factors plays a significant role. However, there is a definite correlation between emotional stress and the formation or aggravation of peptic ulcer disease. It is presumed that emotional stress stimulates the parasympathetic nerve supplying the stomach, which in turn leads to increased secretion of gastric acid and pepsin and to increased stomach motility. Psychological research has attempted to establish a personality profile that predisposes to the development of peptic ulcer disease. Alexander (1950) proposed that people with dependent and help-seeking tendencies are at a higher risk of developing this illness. He suggested that the frustration of such tendencies and the failure to meet dependency needs may activate the parasympathetic system and thus lead to ulcer formation. Recent observations suggest that individuals with characteristics of aggression, sense of urgency, and competitiveness (Type A personality) and those with a limited capacity to express emotions (alexithymics) are more likely to develop peptic ulcer disease. In addition, patients with peptic ulcer disease are more likely to present with symptoms of anxiety and depression as compared with nonulcer patients (McDaniel, Moran, Levenson, & Stoudemire, et al., 1994).

Physical factors that contribute to nonulcer dyspepsia include gastroesophageal reflux, disorders of stomach motility, gastritis, swallowing of excessive amounts of air (aerophagia), and infection with certain bacteria. Neurotic traits, particularly anxiety symptoms, seem to be more common in patients with this condition as compared with other patients (Kellner, 1991).

Treatment Approaches

The treatment of peptic ulcer disease and nonulcer dyspepsias involves complicated medical regimens that are beyond the scope of this book. Psychiatric management, however, can be essential for successful resolution of the illness. Psychotherapy, biofeedback, and behavioral modification may be used separately or in combination for the purpose of stress reduction and pain management. Psychotropic medications, including anxiolytics and antidepressants, may be used if needed.

Prognosis

Peptic ulcer disease may be an acute illness that heals rather rapidly; however, certain cases relapse, leading to chronic ulcers with such complications as intractable pain, nausea, vomiting, bleeding, and perforation, with possible life-threatening consequences. Successful medical treatment together with psychotherapy and relaxation techniques are likely to improve the prognosis significantly.

Nonulcer dyspepsia carries a favorable prognosis, with

the majority of patients becoming symptom-free in a few years. Some patients may later develop peptic ulcer disease. Here, too, the implementation of psychotherapy and behavior modification may improve the chances for complete recovery.

IRRITABLE BOWEL SYNDROME

Clinical Features

Irritable bowel syndrome, which is also known as spastic colitis, presents with symptoms of abdominal pain; altered bowel habit with constipation, diarrhea, or both; and bloating or a feeling of abdominal distension. The pain is likely to be associated with more frequent stool and is often relieved with defecation. In order to make the diagnosis, the symptoms must persist continuously or recur over at least three months. Exclusion of organic pathology is essential. Objective findings include the passage of mucus with the stool, excessively palpable and tender colon, and painful rectal examination.

Irritable bowel syndrome is a relatively common disease that affects between 8 percent and 17 percent of the general population. It can be debilitating and causes significant morbidity. It has been estimated that irritable bowel syndrome ranks second to the common cold as a cause for absenteeism from work. The total annual cost attributable to medical care and loss of productivity in the United States is approximately $1 billion. The disease commonly starts in early adulthood and seems to affect women as often as men (Lydiard, 1992).

Etiology and Contributing Psychological Factors

Among the few physical factors implicated in the etiology of irritable bowel syndrome are abnormal motility or abnormal electrical activity of the colon, increased sensitivity of the bowel to distension, lactose intolerance, and low-residue diet.

There is general agreement among gastroenterologists and psychiatrists that irritable bowel syndrome is greatly influenced by emotional stress. Most studies have consistently demonstrated that patients with the syndrome have substantially more psychiatric disorders than do other patients. Psychiatric disorders commonly found in such patients include Panic Disorder, Generalized Anxiety Disorder, and major depression. On psychological tests and various personality inventories, patients have shown higher scores in the areas of anxiety, depression, and somatization. There is some evidence, as yet inconclusive, that learned behavior originating from early childhood experiences with illness and parents' attitudes toward it may contribute to irritable bowel syndrome (Kellner, 1991). Developmental histories indicate that patients with irritable bowel syndrome made more frequent visits to physicians during childhood as compared with control subjects. Furthermore, loss and separation during early developmental stages often were reported by patients with the syndrome (McDaniel et al., 1994).

Treatment Approaches

The medical management of irritable bowel syndrome consists of dietary discretion, the use of fiber products, the use of antispasmodics, and patient education. The most important aspect of the treatment, however, lies in the successful management of emotional stress. Effective techniques include biofeedback, relaxation training, and hypnosis. Psychotherapy that focuses on explanation, reassurance, and support is also effective. In most patients, the use of anxiolytic agents and antidepressant medications may be needed, especially when symptoms of anxiety or depression are of considerable proportion.

Prognosis

Irritable bowel syndrome tends to become chronic and is characterized by remissions and exacerbations. The symptoms usually relapse following a stressful event. The majority of patients, however, improve with combinations of various treatments (Harvey, Mauad, & Brown, 1987).

ULCERATIVE COLITIS AND REGIONAL ENTERITIS

Clinical Features

Ulcerative colitis is an inflammatory bowel disease involving the colon and the rectum that leads to ulceration, abdominal pain, and severe diarrhea. Rectal bleeding and loss of fluids and electrolytes can cause life-threatening complications. The illness can begin at any age, but it is mostly encountered during the second and third decades of life. It seems to occur in both males and females equally and tends to run in families. The disease is typically chronic, with periods of remission and exacerbation.

Regional enteritis, also known as Crohn's disease, is another related inflammatory bowel disease that involves the colon and the ileum, leading to scarring and perforation of the bowels. Symptoms include abdominal cramping, diarrhea, and weight loss. Although it can occur at any age, its onset is often during the third decade of life, with equal distribution between men and women. Like ulcerative colitis, Crohn's disease is a chronic illness with periods of remission and exacerbation.

Etiology and Contributing Psychological Factors

Inflammatory bowel disease is considered to be an idiopathic condition of an unknown etiology; however, an autoimmune process is probably responsible. Although it has been widely noted in clinical practice that emotional stress is likely to be related to the disease, recent investigations have failed to show a significant relationship between either stressful life events or depression and the subsequent development or exacerbation of inflammatory bowel diseases. Rather, researchers have found that exacerbations of inflammatory bowel disease are likely to be followed by significant depression based on the Beck Depression Inventory (North, Alpers, Helzer, et al., 1991). Unlike patients with irritable bowel syndrome, patients with inflammatory bowel disease do not seem to have a higher incidence of psychiatric diagnoses as compared with control groups—although personality assessment of such patients has indicated the predominance of obsessive-compulsive traits (Olden, 1992). Patients were also found to be hypersensitive to minor issues, such as criticism and rejection. Events that have been described by some patients as occurring prior to the onset of the disease included a significant loss, such as death or separation, or feared threats to an important relationship.

Treatment Approaches

The treatment of inflammatory bowel disease involves complicated medical and surgical interventions that are beyond the scope of this book. Although the simplistic notion that inflammatory bowel disease may be caused by premorbid psychiatric conditions is untenable in contemporary psychiatry, the role of the psychiatrist or the psychotherapist can be of extreme value to the management and success of treatment of this devastating illness. Psychotherapy should be rendered with great caution due to the fragility and sensitivity of these patients. Issues of loss, separation, and rejection should be interpreted gently and skillfully. Psychotropic agents may be used when the clinical presentation warrants their use. Ongoing consultation with the treating gastroenterologist is very important in order to coordinate efforts and communicate clinical progress.

Prognosis

As indicated earlier, inflammatory bowel disease is a chronic illness with periods of remission and exacerbation over many years. Complications include dehydration, bleeding, perforation, and weight loss. The incidence of colon cancer is higher among patients and life expectancy is shortened. Despite current medical therapy, permanent and complete cure is unusual. Surgical removal of the colon may be necessary in certain patients with refractory disease.

10

CARDIOVASCULAR DISORDERS AFFECTED BY PSYCHOLOGICAL FACTORS

The relationship between emotional stress and cardiovascular disorders has long been documented by clinicians and researchers. Psychological factors seem to influence the cardiovascular system in two different ways. First, it is well known that Panic Disorder and Generalized Anxiety Disorder often present with symptoms that resemble classic cardiac symptoms. These symptoms include palpitations, tachycardia, elevated blood pressure, dizziness, chest pain, and difficulty in breathing. Many patients with Panic Disorder or Generalized Anxiety Disorder visit several emergency rooms and many cardiologists' offices before they are accurately diagnosed with the underlying psychiatric condition. Second, the onset and exacerbation of actual cardiovascular diseases, including hypertension and coronary artery disease, have been shown to be heavily influenced by psychological factors and personality traits, as discussed next.

HYPERTENSION

Clinical Features

Hypertension refers to elevation in blood pressure above 140/90. Symptoms include morning headache, dizziness, lightheadedness, and fatigue. It is considered to be one of the leading causes of death for adults and the major risk factor for heart disease and strokes. According to Oparic (1992), it is estimated that over 60 million Americans suffer from hypertension. The disease seems to be twice as common among African Americans as among whites. It occurs more often between ages 25 and 55 and afflicts more women than men.

Etiology and Contributing Psychological Factors

Known causes of hypertension include renal diseases, endocrine disorders, and atherosclerosis, all of which may account for approximately 15 percent of the cases. Almost 85 percent of hypertension cases are classified as "essential hypertension," which refers to nonspecific or unknown etiology.

Emotional factors have been studied in connection with the pathogenesis of essential hypertension. It is commonly known, for example, that emotional stress tends to increase blood pressure. Persons with stressful occupations, such as air traffic controllers, show sustained elevations in blood pressure. Some research has found that certain coping styles, such as excessive expression of anger or inhibited expression of anger may predispose certain individuals to hypertension (McDaniel et al., 1994).

Treatment Approaches

The treatment of hypertension involves complex medical regimens that are beyond the scope of this book. Successful control of hypertension, however, may require the involvement of mental health professionals. Beneficial psychological interventions include biofeedback, relaxation training and various forms of psychotherapy. Psychotropic agents may be used to treat the psychiatric condition, depending on the clinical presentation.

Prognosis

Hypertension is a serious disorder that carries a high degree of morbidity and mortality, especially in untreated cases. The disease is chronic and tends to worsen with age. Serious complications include strokes and cardiac diseases. With proper diet, medical treatment, and psychological interventions, the prognosis can be improved significantly.

CORONARY ARTERY DISEASE

Clinical Features

Coronary artery disease refers to either angina pectoris or myocardial infarction. Symptoms of angina pectoris include chest pain upon exertion, which may be localized or radiate to the jaw, left arm, or other areas. Symptoms of myocardial infarction are chest pain similar to that of angina, along with difficulty in breathing, low blood pressure, or shock. ECG changes, as well as abnormalities in laboratory investigations, are also present. Men are more often affected than women in an overall ratio of 4:1. In men, the peak incidence of symptoms is between ages 50 and 60, whereas in women it is between ages 60 and 70.

Etiology and Contributing Psychological Factors

Coronary artery diseases may be caused by a combination of factors that include age, genetic predisposition, obesity, smoking, and hypertension. Emotional factors that have been shown to contribute to coronary artery disease include Type A behavior pattern, stressful life events, major depression and lack of social support systems (McDaniel et al., 1994).

Treatment Approaches

The treatment of coronary artery diseases includes complicated medical and surgical interventions that can be referred to in medical textbooks. Biofeedback, relaxation techniques, and other behavioral approaches are very effective in controlling hypertension and the progression of coronary artery disease. Psychotherapy for patients with angina can be very helpful as well. Individual supportive psychotherapy and group psychotherapy have been shown to be highly beneficial for victims of myocardial infarction. It is important to encourage the patient to follow an exercise program and resume ordinary activities as soon as possible as advised by physicians. The resumption of normal sexual activity following a heart attack is often feared and thus delayed. Medical evidence suggests that normal sexual activity does not impose any more demand on the heart than does climbing a flight of stairs. Therefore, patients who suffer heart attacks should be educated and encouraged to resume their sexual life. Symptoms of depression and anxiety need to be identified and treated promptly. The use of benzodiazepines or antidepressants may be warranted in some cases (Hackett et al., 1985).

Prognosis

The course of angina pectoris is chronic with intermittent attacks of chest pain, depending on the severity of the obstruction and the degree of exertion. Complications include myocardial infarction and sudden death. Myocardial infarction is often a fatal disease and the prognosis depends largely on early detection and treatment, among several other factors. Complications include heart failure and cardiac arrhythmias. As with hypertension, the psychological interventions outlined are likely to speed the recovery and improve the prognosis.

PSYCHOLOGICAL CONSEQUENCES OF CORONARY ARTERY DISEASES

Patients who suffer from angina pectoris or myocardial infarction often live with the constant fear that they could die at any moment. Although such fear may be medically justified in some instances, many patients tend to exaggerate the fear and become incapacitated by it. Therefore, certain patients with coronary artery diseases may benefit immensely from psychiatric intervention. Support groups, family counseling, and individual psychotherapy can be of great help. It is important for the therapist to understand the actual prognosis well in order to be able to work with such patients. Collaborative consultation with treating physicians and coordination of information given to the patient are extremely important. The focus of therapy must be on education, support, and stress management. In certain cases, where the prognosis is bleak and death is imminent, reality-oriented approaches, along with support to the patient and the family, can prove very helpful.

11

RESPIRATORY DISORDERS AFFECTED BY PSYCHOLOGICAL FACTORS

Like cardiovascular disorders, respiratory diseases are influenced by emotional factors and personality traits. Changes in the rate or depth of breathing, for example, may correlate with different emotional conditions. During anxiety or panic attacks, breathing becomes shallow and rapid, and often the patient experiences difficulty in breathing. In addition, certain respiratory disorders have been known to be aggravated or caused, at least in part, by psychological factors. Such disorders include bronchial asthma, chronic obstructive pulmonary disease, and hyperventilation syndrome.

BRONCHIAL ASTHMA

Clinical Features

Asthma refers to a chronic respiratory disease characterized by episodic or chronic wheezing, difficulty in breathing, cough, and tightness in the chest. The disease occurs more frequently in children, but it can persist through adulthood or begin in adulthood. It is estimated that approximately 3 percent of the population has some form of asthma. Men and women are equally affected by this illness.

Etiology and Contributing Psychological Factors

Asthma is a complex disorder that is believed to be caused by multiple factors involving biochemical, autonomic, immunologic, infectious, endocrine, and psychological etiologies. The basic pathology in asthma is the widespread narrowing of the airways, increased secretion of mucus, airway irritability, and gas exchange abnormalities.

Psychological factors involved in the pathogenesis of asthma have long been documented and studied by clinicians and researchers. Emotional stress is known to exacerbate the symptoms of asthma in most patients. The traditional psychoanalytic views regarding childhood conflicts and actual or anticipated separation or loss during childhood are no longer deemed adequate to account for the psychological mechanisms related to asthma. Current analytically oriented models emphasize the importance of optimal psychophysiological regulatory functions that develop in the process of a successful infant–mother attachment (McDaniel et al., 1994). The failure of such regulatory functions to develop properly may contribute to the onset of asthma in some cases. Furthermore, it has been suggested that certain personality traits and adaptive styles may predispose certain individuals to the onset and recurrence of asthma. Sharma and Nandkumar (1980) proposed that extreme inhibition, covert aggression, and marked dependency needs seem to be highly associated with asthma.

Treatment Approaches

The treatment of asthma involves complicated medical regimens that are tailored to each patient individually,

depending on the severity of the symptoms and the underlying medical condition. Details of such treatments are
available in medical textbooks.

Psychological interventions in asthmatic patients entail
a wide array of therapeutic modalities, including patient
education, stress management, supportive psychotherapy,
and insight-oriented psychotherapy, with a focus on the
free expression of emotions and changing maladaptive
behavior.

Prognosis

In general, the prognosis for asthma is excellent with
modern treatment. Most asthmatic children recover fully
and do not experience any further attacks during adulthood. However, some do continue to suffer from recurrent
attacks throughout their life. Complications of asthma
include airway infection, dehydration, syncope, cardiac
enlargement, and hypoxia. The mortality rate is about 0.1
percent. Asthmatic attacks can be minimized by eliminat-
ing external factors that trigger the attacks, by early treatment of respiratory infections, and by discontinuation of
cigarette smoking.

CHRONIC OBSTRUCTIVE PULMONARY DISEASE

Clinical Features

Chronic obstructive pulmonary disease (COPD) refers to
chronic cough and sputum production, difficulty in breathing, wheezing, and reduced airflow into the lungs. It is
estimated that about 10 million Americans suffer from some
degree of COPD. The age of onset is typically in the fifth or
sixth decade of life, and the symptoms persist for years.

Etiology and Contributing Psychological Factors

Chronic obstructive pulmonary disease is caused by either
chronic bronchitis or emphysema. Most patients with

COPD have features of both conditions. Chronic smoking seems to be a significant factor in causing chronic bronchitis and emphysema leading to COPD. Other causes include air pollution, chronic respiratory infection, allergy, and familial factors.

The impact of emotional stress on COPD has been documented by clinicians and researchers. There are no specific psychological or personality factors that seem to contribute to its exacerbation. However, Burns and Howell (1969) suggested that exaggeration of difficulty in breathing is encountered more often in patients with depression, Anxiety Disorder, and histrionic personality traits.

Treatment Approaches

The medical management of COPD is complicated and beyond the scope of this book, but the role of mental health professionals in this regard can be important. It is critical to identify stressful events that exacerbate the symptoms and to help the patient develop coping strategies for dealing with them. Treatment of underlying Anxiety Disorder and depression can greatly improve the physical condition. Psychotropic agents may be used with caution in some situations. Lorazepam may be helpful in patients whose anxiety level is such that it interferes with their ability to breathe. Family therapy may be needed in certain cases where there is significant avoidance or denial of intense affect. Family sessions should focus on the family members' helplessness and anger, especially in cases of ventilator-dependent patients (McDaniel et al., 1994).

Prognosis

The outlook for patients with COPD is generally poor. This illness is usually progressive and does not respond well to treatment, although successful treatment may prolong life and slow the rate of decline of pulmonary function. Cessation of cigarette smoking, early treatment of airway infections, and vaccination against influenza and pneumonia may be of benefit in this regard. Complications include pneumonia, pulmonary embolisms, respiratory failure, and heart failure. In addition, reduced oxygen concentration can lead to memory deficit and other cognitive impairment, particularly in elderly patients.

Psychological interventions may be helpful in terminal stages for both the patient and the family. The absence of preexisting psychopathology, patient education, and optimism improve the prognosis.

HYPERVENTILATION SYNDROME

Clinical Features

Hyperventilation syndrome refers to a state of rapid breathing resulting in a tingling sensation, numbness, muscle spasm, buzzing in the ears, blurred vision, feelings of derealization, lightheadedness, dizziness, and faintness. Uncontrollable laughter or crying may occur. The exact prevalence of this condition is not known, however, studies estimate it to range between 13 percent and 40 percent, depending on coexisting psychiatric disorders (Kellner, 1991). The syndrome occurs most often between 15 and 30 years of age and is more common in women than in men.

Etiology and Contributing Psychological Factors

Several physical illnesses are capable of producing excessive and rapid breathing patterns. These include pulmonary edema, pulmonary embolism, respiratory diseases, hypoglycemia, salicylate poisoning, and central nervous system lesions. These conditions need to be differentiated from psychosomatic hyperventilation, which is the focus of this section.

Psychological causes of hyperventilation syndrome include fear, Anxiety Disorder, panic attacks, and hysteria. Certain patients, especially those with histrionic personality organization, may react to stressful situations by hyperventilating and possibly fainting.

Treatment Approaches

Hyperventilation attacks can be treated by allowing the patient to continue to breathe inside a paper bag in order to increase the concentration of carbon dioxide in the blood and restore acid-base balance. Patients may be trained to control their breathing utilizing certain behavioral techniques. Tranquilizers, such as Valium, can help relax the patient and reduce the rate of respiration. Psychiatric follow-up is important to identify and treat underlying anxiety or panic attacks and resolve psychological conflicts.

Prognosis

Hyperventilation syndrome carries a favorable prognosis, with no impairment to physical health in most cases. The condition, however, is distressing and can reoccur over a long time. The ultimate prognosis depends largely on the treatment outcome of the underlying psychiatric condition.

PSYCHOLOGICAL CONSEQUENCES OF CHRONIC RESPIRATORY DISEASES

Patients with chronic respiratory diseases often live with fear and constant anxiety as they perceive their disabling illness to be life threatening. Although in many patients this reaction is justifiable and based on medical facts, in others, the fear and anxiety may be exaggerated considering the actual prognosis. Unfortunately, in these patients a vicious cycle develops where dyspnea generates anxiety and fear, and then anxiety itself leads to further impairment in breathing capacity or hyperventilation. Education, support groups, and individual psychotherapy can be of great help to many patients. Selective use of anxiolytic agents and other psychotropic medications may be needed in some cases.

12

DERMATOLOGICAL DISORDERS AFFECTED BY PSYCHOLOGICAL FACTORS

The skin plays a central role in social interaction among people, being the most immediately visible aspect of one's appearance. Most often, and under normal circumstances, emotional reactions become manifest in changes in the skin. For example, an embarrassing situation may cause a person to blush and a frightening circumstance may cause one to become pale and perspire. Skin disfigurement due to burns or disease can have a great impact on the psychological makeup of the individual, and hence on interpersonal relationships. Skin disease may cause serious emotional difficulty, including shame, social withdrawal, and depression. Certain pathological skin conditions can be triggered or exacerbated by emotional stress. These include psoriasis, dermatitis, acne, urticaria, pruritus, and alopecia areata.

PSORIASIS

Psoriasis is a chronic inflammatory skin disease that shows up as silvery scales on bright red plaques on the knees, elbows, and scalp. The exact cause of psoriasis is not known, however, genetic and immunologic factors have been suggested. The disease is fairly common and affects approximately three million individuals in the United States alone.

The disease tends to flare up during periods of emotional stress, yet no specific psychological conflict or personality type seems to be more common among patients predisposed to psoriasis. As expected, the visible disfigurement that may be caused by the disease can lead to serious psychological reactions in victims. Most patients become self-conscious and anticipate rejection and avoidance by others. This often leads to social withdrawal and deterioration of interpersonal relationships, which in turn deprives the patient of help and support (Ramsay & O'Reagan, 1988).

DERMATITIS

Atopic dermatitis or eczema is an allergic skin disease that causes an itchy rash, which may appear on almost any part of the body. The exact cause of atopic dermatitis is not known, however, genetic and immunologic factors are involved. Affective disorders, migraine headaches, and irritable bowel syndrome seem to occur in association with dermatitis, suggesting that the neurotransmitter serotonin may play a role (Garvey & Tollefson, 1988). Many patients with atopic dermatitis show signs of hungering for affection and physical closeness and have a history of emotional deprivation early in life (Engels, 1985).

Like psoriasis, dermatitis may become worse when there is emotional stress. Severe cases can cause disfiguring skin lesions, leading to social withdrawal and serious psychological complications.

ACNE

Acne is a common inflammatory skin disease involving the sebaceous glands of the face, back, and shoulders. The disease affects primarily the adolescent population, but it may persist through the sixth decade of life. The primary cause of acne seems to be related to hormonal factors. Genetic and dietary factors may be involved as well.

Most patients with acne report exacerbation of their condition during periods of emotional stress. Severe cases of acne can cause serious scarring and skin disfigurement with major social and psychological consequences. Several psychological studies of patients with acne reveal a high prevalence of emotional problems. Poor self-esteem and negative self-image have been reported frequently among acne patients. Furthermore, studies have demonstrated that successful treatment of severe acne can result in reduction of anxiety and depression (Rubinow, Peck, Squillace, et al., 1987).

URTICARIA

Urticaria refers to cutaneous eruptions of hives or wheals that often lead to severe itching. The condition is invariably self-limited and often disappears within 24 hours, although certain cases may last for one or two weeks. The cause is believed to be immunologic, with a complicated mechanism.

Psychological factors, such as severe anxiety reactions, have been implicated in the etiology of urticaria. Personality types that have been described in association with this condition include those of repressed aggressiveness, infantile qualities, and masochistic behavioral patterns (Engels, 1985).

PRURITUS

Pruritus or itching can be caused by a wide variety of skin disorders. However, in certain situations, itching may occur in the absence of any skin disease or allergy. Psychogenic causes of pruritus have been observed and studied by various researchers and clinicians. Anxious and tense individuals may experience itching sensations and attempt to scratch various areas of the body. Other psychological reactions have been shown to trigger itching, including repressed anger, repressed anxiety, guilt, and sexual arousal. Itching and the subsequent scratching may be perceived as pleasurable by most individuals, especially when involving the genital areas.

Patients with chronic psychogenic pruritus should be evaluated for underlying psychological conflict and should receive appropriate psychological counseling.

ALOPECIA AREATA

Alopecia areata refers to patchy scalp hair loss that occurs in certain individuals for unknown reasons. Emotional stress has been identified as a causative factor in many cases of alopecia areata. Loss or threat of abandonment early in life may be a contributing factor. Psychoneuroimmunologic components may be at play in the pathogenesis of this condition (Engels, 1985).

CLINICAL IMPLICATIONS OF
DERMATOLOGICAL DISORDERS

As most skin disorders are likely to cause disfiguring lesions, serious psychological sequelae can be expected, as discussed previously. Psychiatric intervention may be helpful in some cases in order to minimize social withdrawal and improve interpersonal contact. Supportive psychotherapy, encouragement, and stress management can be beneficial. Severe depression or anxiety may require administration of psychotropic agents.

13

THE ROLE OF PSYCHOLOGICAL FACTORS IN IMMUNE DISORDERS AND CANCER

PSYCHOIMMUNOLOGY

Clinicians have long known that emotional factors play an important role in several immune disorders. Recent advances in the understanding of the chemistry of the brain and the interrelationship among the nervous, the endocrine, and the immune systems through the interaction of various neurotransmitters have shed more light on those early observations and have enhanced our appreciation of the mind–body connection. It is well documented that the brain interacts with and modulates various immunologic systems, a relationship that is discussed in the following.

Theoretical Considerations

It has been known for a long time that the central nervous system supplies nerves to various immune organs, such as the thymus gland, the spleen, and lymph nodes. A number

of investigators have demonstrated the existence of anatomical and neurohormonal connections between the brain
and the immune system. Recent research has documented
that cells of the immune system contain receptors for
various neurotransmitters, neurohormones, and neuropeptides (Gorman & Kertzner, 1990). Consequently, and since
it has been shown that psychological factors can influence
the interaction among various neurotransmitter systems, it
is only logical to conclude that such psychological factors
are likely to influence the immune systems as well, leading
to altered immune responses in both normal individuals
and patients. Evidence from human studies suggests that
severe psychosocial stress can decrease the defensive
capacity of the body and hence can increase the likelihood
of developing infection by a number of bacteria and
viruses (Knapp, 1985).

Clinical Implications

There have been numerous publications documenting the
effect of bereavement on immunity. Researchers have
shown that immune responses were decreased among
recently bereaved individuals and among others with
anticipatory bereavement (Irwin, Daniel, Smith, et al.,
1987). On the other hand, studies of patients with Depressive Disorders showed inconsistent results; in some, immune responses were decreased, whereas in others, immune
responses were normal (Stein, Miller, & Trestman, 1991).
Other conditions that seem to reduce immune responses
include severely stressful events, such as work-related
stress, final examinations, and going though a divorce
(McDaniel et al., 1994).

Treatment Approaches

It has been shown that patients who are experiencing or
anticipating bereavement and those who are depressed
can benefit from psychological interventions, particularly

group therapy. The value of such treatment goes beyond support, minimizing the unwarranted effects that such stressful events can impose on the immune system. Reducing the stress level, improving coping mechanisms, and promoting hope and a positive attitude may enhance the body's natural defenses against infections, cancer, and disease in general, although definite scientific proof is still lacking.

RHEUMATOID ARTHRITIS

The assertion made by Alexander (1950) and others that rheumatoid arthritis is one of the major psychosomatic disorders has been challenged, and the condition is now seen mainly as an autoimmune disorder. However, there is a general agreement among patients and physicians that emotional stress tends to aggravate the symptoms of rheumatoid arthritis. Recent evidence has shown that up to 50 percent of patients with rheumatoid arthritis appear depressed on psychological testing. Anxiety and depression seem to affect the patient's capacity and will for long-term compliance with treatment, and, consequently, may contribute to treatment failure and poor prognosis. In order to ensure good treatment outcome, it is essential to evaluate the effectiveness of the support system and to encourage the patient's family and friends to become involved in the treatment process. Depression, frustration, and psychological withdrawal can lead to increased physical withdrawal, increased pain, and increased use of analgesics (McDaniel et al., 1994).

PSYCHOONCOLOGY

The work in the field of psychoneuroimmunology and the recent findings suggesting that psychological factors can influence the course and outcome of immunological disorders has focused the attention of both clinicians and researchers on a similar relationship between cancer and emotional factors. This is not surprising as many experts believe that at least certain types of cancer are related to immunological mechanisms. Weakened immunity in AIDS patients, for example, invites the growth of certain kinds of tumors. Furthermore, certain new treatment approaches to cancer utilize immune systems to attack cancerous cells. Therefore, as with immune disorders, emotional factors may play a significant role in malignant disorders.

Theoretical Considerations

Although there is clear evidence suggesting that psychological factors do indeed influence the onset and progression of cancer in some patients, the exact mechanism involved in this process is not clearly understood. There have been some studies that demonstrated that individuals who tend to be unassertive, compliant with external authorities, and suppress negative emotions are at a higher risk for developing cancer. Evidence taken from several animal experiments suggests that psychosocial factors in many species can lead to increased susceptibility to malignant growth or decreased ability to survive malignant implants or both (Knapp, 1985). As indicated, it is likely that the immune system is the key factor in this regard. Several other unknown factors are probably at play as well.

Clinical Implications

Numerous studies have suggested that emotional factors and stressful life experiences, such as separation or loss, often precede the clinical onset of various types of cancer. In a recent prospective study that lasted for eight years, Geyer (1991) demonstrated that an increased incidence of stressful events was significantly correlated with the onset of breast cancer among women. Greer, Morris, and

Pettingale (1979) reported that breast cancer patients who had a "fighting spirit" or those who employed denial as defense mechanism had a higher survival rate as compared with those patients who accepted their fate and expressed hopelessness and helplessness.

In a 17-year follow-up epidemiological study, Shekelle, Raynor, and Ostfeld (1981) reported that individuals with depressive symptoms had a higher-than-normal incidence of various types of cancer and had twice as high a risk of death from cancer. Recent studies have failed to show such a significant correlation between depression and cancer. Furthermore, the correlation between bereavement and the onset of cancer among survivors remains controversial (McDaniel et al., 1994).

Treatment Approaches

Several recent studies have demonstrated that group therapy is very effective for cancer patients. Fawzy, Cousins, Fawzy, et al. (1990), and Fawzy, Kemeny, Fawzy, et al. 1990) studied a group of postsurgical patients with malignant melanoma and did a comparison between patients who received group therapy and those who did not. Patients who received group therapy showed less psychological distress, more effective coping, and increased immune response and natural defense against the cancer. Spiegel, Bloom, Kramer, et al. (1989) also demonstrated that group therapy coupled with self-hypnosis among women with metastatic breast cancer led to reduction in pain and distress and prolonged survival rate.

Other psychiatric and psychological interventions, including individual psychotherapy, family therapy, cognitive therapy, relaxation techniques, and other behavioral methods, can be of great value. In addition, psychopharmacological interventions in cases of severe depression or anxiety may be essential.

Mental health professionals who work with cancer patients need to consider the influence of psychological factors on the course of cancer with caution. It is important to keep in mind that despite advanced therapies, cancer remains one of the most serious and potentially fatal diseases. Although psychological interventions may be helpful in some patients, their effectiveness with regard to the final prognosis of the cancer may be minimal. The positive outcome of the studies cited here and other clinical examples where patients are reported to have "beaten" the cancer should not be overstated or viewed in a simplistic fashion. It is important, however, to provide the patient with education, support, and encouragement in order to "fight" the cancer, keeping in mind that aggressive medical treatments should always be the main intervention. The therapist needs to remain objective concerning the prognosis and the realistic chances for survival. Family therapy may be beneficial in certain cases, especially for patients with terminal cancer.

14

PSYCHOLOGICAL FACTORS AFFECTING HEADACHES AND MIGRAINE

DEFINITIONS AND CLINICAL FEATURES

Headache is an extremely common symptom with numerous etiological factors that are beyond the scope of this book. However, several types of headaches have been described as being associated, at least in part, with emotional factors, including tension headache, posttraumatic headache, and migraine.

Tension headache is often described by patients as a painful tightening band that surrounds the entire head, leading to constant daily headache. The pain may be exacerbated by emotional stress, fatigue, noise, or glare. The attack occurs more often toward the end of the day or in early evening. This type of headache is very common, occurring in about 80 percent of the population during periods of emotional stress. Symptoms of anxiety and depression are frequently reported by patients with tension headache.

Posttraumatic headache occurs in some patients following a closed head injury. Often, other neurological signs are lacking and the clinical features of the headache do not correlate with the severity of the original injury. It is believed that this type of headache is mainly psychogenic. Clinical features of posttraumatic headache are variable and nonspecific. Cognitive impairment, irritability, and depression may be present. Malingering for the purpose of secondary gain or litigation may be involved in some cases.

Migraine headache is defined as a lateralized throbbing headache that is severe in nature and may be accompanied by nausea, vomiting, photophobia, and blurring of vision. Visual hallucinations and other neurological manifestations may occur as well. The headache usually builds up gradually and may last for several hours or days. The attack may be triggered by emotional or physical stress, lack of sleep, certain foods, alcohol, birth control pills, or the onset of menstruation. The family history is often positive.

ETIOLOGY AND CONTRIBUTING FACTORS

Several medical conditions can cause different types of headache, which may be referred to in medical textbooks. Tension headaches are often caused by prolonged contraction of head and neck muscles, usually following stressful events, anxiety, or depression. Migraine headaches are due to vascular constriction and dilation and are also triggered by emotional or physical stress.

Psychogenic causes of headaches include chronic anxiety and depression. Headache may be reported frequently in the course of various Somatoform Disorders, including Somatization Disorder, Conversion Disorder, and hypochondriasis.

Migraine and depression seem to share an important biological abnormality. In both conditions, it has been demonstrated that serotonin levels are decreased (Glover, Jarman, & Sandler, 1993). This overlap may account for the fact that both conditions respond to antidepressant medications that increase serotonin levels.

PSYCHOLOGICAL THEORIES

Clinical and research findings suggest that headaches and migraine are associated with a high incidence of psychiatric disorders. Psychological factors, such as severe emotional stress, anxiety, depression, personality style, and stressful life events, seem to be highly correlated with the severity and persistence of headaches (Shulman, 1991). Personality traits that seem to correlate with frequent headaches include inadequacy and rigidity (Passchier, Schouten, Van-der-Donk, & Van-Romunde, 1991).

PATIENT EVALUATION

Patients with chronic headaches are often referred to a mental health professional after it has been determined by the internist or the neurologist that emotional factors are involved in the etiology or persistence. It is important to confirm that all physical causes have been ruled out. A thorough psychiatric history and a detailed mental status examination need to be performed in order to assess the possible coexistence of psychiatric disorders. It is equally important to acknowledge the validity of the pain endured by the patient even though it is primarily caused by emotional factors. The patient must be told that the headache he or she is experiencing is real, but that it is likely to be worsened by stress. Most patients will agree with the therapists in this regard. Patients need to be educated and informed that psychological stress can lead to physical changes, such as muscle contraction and chemical changes that in turn can contribute to the headache. This step is important in order to engage the patient in psychiatric treatment and to make optimal progress.

TREATMENT APPROACHES

Various medical interventions for pain management, including the use of painkillers and other pain management techniques, are usually implemented before the patient is referred to mental health professionals (Chapter 5). Psychiatric diagnosis and treatment often add a very useful and important dimension to the medical care of the headache patient (Shulman, 1991).

The use of anxiolytic agents and antidepressants can be critical in certain patients. Tricyclic antidepressants, particularly amitriptyline (Elavil) and nortriptyline (Pamelor), seem to possess an analgesic effect at small doses. Higher doses may be needed for antidepressant effect. Modern antidepressants, which are known as selective serotonin reuptake inhibitors (SSRIs), such as Prozac, Zoloft, and Paxil, can be very effective in both depression and migraines. Prolonged use of benzodiazepines should be avoided whenever possible because of potential dependency problems.

The most effective psychiatric interventions for the management of chronic headaches and migraine include patient education, relaxation techniques, biofeedback, hypnotherapy, and stress training (Chapter 5). These techniques can be used separately or in various combinations with good results. Individual psychotherapy and support groups may be beneficial as well. Combinations of psychotropic medications with nonpharmacological modalities such as those just outlined often yield the greatest clinical outcome (Andrasik, 1990).

PROGNOSIS

Tension headaches and migraines tend to be chronic and difficult to treat. The success of the treatment in certain cases depends largely on identifying and treating underlying psychiatric disorders. It also depends on the patient's ability to adapt and to cope with chronic pain. It is important to emphasize that suicidal ideation as well as suicide attempts can occur in the course of migraine and coexisting major depression (Breslau, 1992). Therefore, vigorous steps should be taken to treat the depression in such individuals.

Posttraumatic headache also tends to be chronic and may be difficult to treat. Issues of secondary gain or litigation in cases of automobile accidents and work-related head injuries may contribute to the protracted course of the headache and need to be addressed during treatment.

15

THE ROLE OF PSYCHOLOGICAL FACTORS IN OBESITY

DEFINITION AND CLINICAL FEATURES

Obesity may be defined as excessive accumulation of body fat leading to weight greater than 20 percent above the ideal weight, as indicated in the standard height–weight tables (Bray, 1978). According to this definition, close to a quarter of the U.S. population would be considered obese. Obesity is more common in women than in men, and tends to be more prevalent among people of lower socioeconomic status. Most obese individuals seem to have great difficulty in restraining their eating behavior and in achieving satiety. In addition, some individuals report increased eating during dysphoric states or emotional upset (Halmi, 1994).

CAUSES

It is accepted among clinicians and researchers that obesity is caused by multiple factors.

Biological Factors

Eating behavior seems to be controlled by complex neural mechanisms involving several neurotransmitters, neuropeptides, and opioids within the hypothalamus and other areas in the brain. Lipid, amino acid, and glucose metabolism all seem to be involved in a feedback mechanism to central neural regulatory functions that influence eating behavior (Halmi, 1994). It is conceivable that disruption in the regulatory functions described is likely to cause abnormal eating behavior.

Genetic Factors

Obesity has a definite familial component, suggesting a genetic etiology. Recent research findings have supported this hypothesis, at least in certain individuals. Eighty percent of the offspring of two obese parents are likely to become obese, as compared with 40 percent of the offspring when one parent is obese. Only 10 percent of the offspring of nonobese patents are likely to become obese (Halmi, 1994).

Medical Factors

It is important to keep in mind that certain forms of obesity may be associated with specific medical conditions, such as brain damage in the hypothalamic area, hypothyroidism, Cushing's syndrome, and other endocrine disorders.

Physical Activity

It is generally known that obese individuals are less active than are normal-weight people. Physical activity increases caloric expenditure, and hence prevents the accumulation of fat. Furthermore, physical activity may decrease food intake and prevent the fall in metabolic rate that often accompanies dieting (Halmi, 1994).

Eating Habits

Cultural and environmental influences seem to play a major role in obesity. Overeating habits reinforced by families and some cultures may contribute to excessive weight gain. On one level, it seems obvious that overeating leads to the accumulation of more calories than the body needs to expend as energy; however, it is not always as simple to assume that obesity can be prevented by dietary restriction. Obese individuals tend to binge eat when subjected to severe emotional stress. Bulimic behavior may also occur.

Emotional Factors

Although it is widely thought that emotional stress leads to increased overeating, a review of the literature conducted by Allison and Heshka (1993) raised some questions about the validity of that notion. Christensen (1993) concluded that food may be viewed as a regulator of negative mood states. He elaborated that individuals abstaining from use of tobacco or alcohol tend to consume more carbohydrates to lift their negative mood state. He added that individuals with Seasonal Affective Disorder or premenstrual syndrome, and depressed obese patients crave and increase their consumption of carbohydrates, which may lead to heightened energy and a lifting of depression. A possible mechanism for this action may be due to the effect of carbohydrate ingestion on central serotonin synthesis and release.

Most studies show that there is no distinct or excess psychopathology or specific personality profile among obese individuals. However, patients who seek treatment for obesity may show a higher incidence of psychopathology as compared with other medical or surgical patients (O'Neil & Jarrell, 1992). Major depression appears to be common among such individuals, although this diagnosis is no more prevalent in obese patients than in the general population.

Individuals who have been obese since childhood are particularly hurt by stigmatization and prejudice and tend to develop symptoms of depression and anxiety. There is also some evidence that obese individuals may face discrimination in the areas of education and employment (Halmi, 1994).

TREATMENT APPROACHES

In addition to traditional treatments consisting of diet and exercise, several psychological treatments seem to improve the chance of weight reduction and the sustainment of lower weight.

Behavior Therapy

Behavior analysis must be conducted in order to prescribe effective behavior therapy techniques. Programs include self-monitoring, nutrition education, physical activity, and cognitive restructuring. Behavioral therapies in most clinical studies have shown clear superiority over other treatment modalities.

Psychotherapy

Individual psychotherapy may not be indicated for the purpose of treating obesity unless significant psychopathology can be identified. The effectiveness of this modality may be enhanced when combined with other treatments.

Group Therapy

Several forms of self-help groups exist to deal with eating behavior and issues of obesity. Although these groups appear to be helpful, it is difficult to assess their effectiveness accurately because of very high dropout rates.

Pharmacological Treatment

Drugs that curb the appetite, including phenylpropanol-amine hydrochloride, fenfluramine hydrochloride, and other amphetamine derivatives, may be used in some patients. However, it must be kept in mind that upon discontinuation of such agents it is likely that a rebound weight gain, along with lethargy and depression, may occur.

Psychotropic agents, particularly antidepressant medications, may be used, depending on clinical indications and the symptoms that may accompany obesity. It is important to note here that some antidepressant medications and other psychotropic agents could also contribute to weight gain. Furthermore, and contrary to some claims, no particular antidepressant has been shown to cause weight loss.

Surgery

In cases of severe obesity where the weight increase exceeds 100 percent of the normal weight, surgical procedures may be required. Such procedures include reduction of the size of the stomach, intestinal bypass, and removal of excess fat. Surgical treatments for some patients may offer significant improvements in self-esteem, marital satisfaction, and social adjustment.

COMPLICATIONS AND PROGNOSIS

Medical complications include high blood pressure, increased risk for heart disease, respiratory problems, arthritis, diabetes mellitus, and increased risk for certain types of cancer. In general, the mortality rate is likely to increase with obesity (Halmi, 1994).

Psychological complications include bulimic behavior consisting of binge eating followed by purging, depression, and self-deprecating thoughts. Obese individuals encounter serious social criticism and rejection, which may lead to withdrawal and resentment. Some obese individuals may develop disparagement of the body image, feeling that their bodies are grotesque and loathsome and that people view them with hostility and contempt. This feeling may lead to self-consciousness and impairment in social functioning.

Anxiety and depression may be seen in obese individuals and appropriate interventions should be made to correct the problems. Sexual dysfunction and marital difficulties are likely to arise as consequences of obesity as well.

16

FIBROMYALGIA

DEFINITION AND CLINICAL FEATURES

Fibromyalgia, also known as fibrositis, refers to a clinical syndrome consisting of chronic widespread muscular aches and pains, stiffness, fatigue, multiple trigger points (tender spots at various anatomical sites), and a characteristic sleep disturbance. Other complaints include swelling and numbness, and pain in the neck and shoulders. Headache, irritable bowel syndrome, and interstitial cystitis (urinary bladder condition) are often associated with fibromyalgia (Yunus, 1989; Buchwald & Garrity, 1994).

This is a relatively common syndrome with a prevalence rate in rheumatology clinics of 15 percent to 20 percent. The syndrome occurs most commonly in young, well-educated women. The female-to-male ratio is about five to one (Kellner, 1991).

ETIOLOGY AND CONTRIBUTING FACTORS

It is essential to note here that in fibromyalgia, all laboratory investigations, including sedimentation rate, muscle enzyme level, rheumatic factors, and antinuclear antibody, are usually within normal limits, as compared with other rheumatological disorders. This fact has raised the question as to whether this entity is a true rheumatic syndrome or a Psychosomatic Disorder, perhaps related to Depressive Disorders.

A metabolic etiology for fibromyalgia has been proposed on the basis that patients with severe forms have low
levels of free tryptophan (a precursor of serotonin). This
may account for reduced pain threshold and non-REM
sleep disturbances in fibromyalgia patients (Kellner, 1991).
Furthermore, it has long been established that low serotonin levels are associated with depression, which is common in fibromyalgia patients.

Genetic factors may be involved in the etiology of
fibromyalgia. A dominant autosomal inheritance pattern
has been proposed. First-degree relatives of patients with
fibromyalgia frequently demonstrate depressive characteristics.

At this point, there is no convincing theory to account
for the etiology of fibromyalgia. Kellner (1991) suggested
that a combination of factors, including physical disease,
psychopathology, and low serotonin concentration, may
lead to abnormalities involving stage 4 sleep. This in turn
decreases the pain threshold and induces various symptoms of fibromyalgia. He added that other unknown hormonal, biochemical, or immune mechanisms also may be
involved.

PSYCHOLOGICAL ASPECTS

The role of psychological factors in the etiology of
fibromyalgia has been controversial. Several studies have
been conducted to evaluate patients with fibromyalgia and
compare them with other patients, utilizing various inventories and scales. Fibromyalgia patients who attended
rheumatology clinics were shown to have more psychopathology as compared with other patients and with control
subjects. Most researchers and clinicians agree that emotional distress and depressive affect seem to be common
among almost all patients with fibromyalgia.

In a recent blinded controlled study conducted by Krag,
Norregaard, Larsen, et al. (1994), patients with fibromyalgia

were compared with a control group of other rheumatologic patients with pain. The fibromyalgia patients scored higher on both anxiety and depression scales, again confirming earlier findings.

DIAGNOSTIC CONSIDERATIONS

Diagnosis can be made based on the history of chronic musculoskeletal aches and stiffness with tender points, impaired sleep pattern, and other associated symptoms as described. Conventionally, the diagnosis of fibromyalgia is not made unless the symptoms have persisted for at least three months. Furthermore, many rheumatologists require a minimum of eight tender points to make the diagnosis. Most laboratory investigations are typically normal in most patients with fibromyalgia, despite the morbid clinical picture (Kellner, 1991).

TREATMENT APPROACHES

The treatment of fibromyalgia can be difficult, lengthy, and frustrating due to the relatively poor response to various treatment modalities. For this reason, it is always advisable to use a combination of treatments as outlined below.

Drug Therapy

Numerous drugs have been used in the treatment of fibromyalgia, including nonsteroidal anti-inflammatory agents, nonnarcotic analgesics, corticosteroids, and hypnotics. The benefits of these drugs are limited and vary from one patient to another.

Sedating, serotonergically active antidepressants, such as doxipen, amitriptyline, or nortriptyline, are often helpful and are considered to be the drugs of choice (Goldenberg, 1986). Antidepressant medications appear to be beneficial to fibromyalgia patients, even in the absence of major depression. The relatively new class of antidepressants known as SSRIs (Prozac, Zoloft, and Paxil) has shown good effect in some fibromyalgia patients. In addition, the new antidepressant Effexor (venlafaxine HCl) has been used with some success.

Other drugs that have been shown to be more effective than placebo include cyclobenzaprine (Flexeril) and a homeopathic remedy known as RHUS TOXICODENDRON (Fisher, Greenwood, Huskisson, et al., 1989).

Trigger Point Injection

Injection of local anesthetics into tender points has proved effective as shown by several studies (Fine, Milano, & Hard, 1988). The treatment may be repeated over several weeks or months.

Biofeedback

Electromyographic biofeedback seemed to be effective in some fibromyalgia patients, especially those with no overt psychopathology. In this technique, patients are instructed to relax and receive a signal indicating the degree of relaxation. Ferraccioli, Ghirelli, Scita, et al. (1987) reported that the treated group showed a substantial improvement in tender points, pain, and morning stiffness as compared with the control group.

Physical Therapy and Exercise

Most studies have demonstrated that physical therapy, rehabilitation programs, and various fitness exercises provide significant relief for symptoms of muscle aches, stiffness, and tender points.

Psychotherapy

The role of psychotherapy in the treatment of fibromyalgia is very important, especially in patients with a high degree of psychopathology, including Anxiety and Depressive Disorders. A combination of supportive, cognitive, and behavioral techniques offers the best results and accelerates the recovery. Patient education and preparation for realistic prognosis are essential parts of the therapeutic process.

Other Treatments

Other therapeutic modalities have also been used in the treatment of fibromyalgia with mixed results. These include massage therapy, heat therapy, cold therapy, ultrasound, transcutaneous electrical nerve stimulation (TENS), ethylchloride spray, and acupuncture (McCain, 1989).

COURSE AND PROGNOSIS

About six percent of the patients with fibromyalgia consider themselves disabled due to several factors, including emotional stress, fatigue, sleep disturbances, and isolated lifestyle (Buchwald & Garrity, 1994). Patients tend to miss work and seek frequent medical treatment. The patient is often despondent over the lack of progress despite various treatments and may become angry and doubtful about recovery.

The long-term prognosis depends on the nature, duration, and severity of the disorder. According to Masi and Yunus (1986), four different categories of patients seem to be encountered in clinical settings. Some patients recover after one attack, with no subsequent episodes; others have an intermittent course, with periods of remission and exacerbation; another group has a fluctuating course, but with some pain even between attacks; and a final group of patients report constant symptoms and sustain a nonremitting course.

17

CHRONIC FATIGUE
SYNDROME

DEFINITION AND CLINICAL FEATURES

Chronic fatigue syndrome was defined originally by Holmes, Kaplan, Gantz, et al. (1988) as chronic or recurrent debilitating fatigue, which is aggravated after exertion and lasts for at least six months. Associated features may include sore throat, headache, muscle pain, joint pain, decreased memory, poor concentration, confusion, and depression. Patients may feel that they have fever, and lymph node tenderness may be present. Typically, physical examination and laboratory investigations are normal. There are no accurate data with regard to the prevalence of chronic fatigue syndrome in the general population, however, it is more common in women and has its onset following a "flulike illness" (Buchwald & Garrity, 1994).

DIFFERENTIAL DIAGNOSIS

Chronic fatigue syndrome needs to be differentiated from chronic fatigue, which is limited to a pervasive feeling of being tired in the absence of the other associated features. In addition, several medical conditions need to be ruled out in patients who report chronic fatigue. These include malignancies, infections (including HIV), autoimmune diseases, endocrine disorders, drug abuse, and cardiac or pulmonary diseases (Holmes et al., 1988). In most of these conditions, physical examination and laboratory investigations often show specific abnormalities.

It is important to note here that patients' characteristics and several of the symptoms encountered in chronic fatigue syndrome are very similar to those present in fibromyalgia and vice versa, suggesting that the conditions may be similar in many ways (Buchwald & Garrity, 1994).

ETIOLOGY AND PATHOPHYSIOLOGY

To date, no definitive etiological factor has been identified as being responsible for the disease, although several hypotheses have been proposed. The main theory suggests that the syndrome may be caused by a viral infection. Serological testing has supported this theory in some patients. Other theories have suggested that metabolic abnormalities and defective immune regulation may also be involved. In addition, some researchers have noted that permanent cognitive impairment and depressive symptoms might implicate neuropsychological deficits as being responsible for the syndrome (Kellner, 1991).

On the other hand, several clinicians and researchers have suggested that chronic fatigue syndrome may in fact represent a variant of Depressive Disorders with particular features. This point remains controversial, although most patients with chronic fatigue syndrome share many common symptoms with depressed patients, and both groups benefit from antidepressant medications.

PSYCHOLOGICAL FACTORS

Most recent studies (Manu, Matthews, & Lane, 1988) have shown that several psychiatric disorders can be associated with fatigue, including major depression, dysthymia, Anxiety Disorder, Somatization Disorder, and emotional stress. The term "neurasthenia," which was commonly used in the psychiatric literature in the past, certainly refers to many of the features described in chronic fatigue syndrome. Although the term is not included in DSM-IV, it has been retained by ICD-10. No particular personality traits or specific psychological profiles have been identified in connection with the chronic fatigue syndrome.

TREATMENT APPROACHES

In cases where a specific etiology can be identified, appropriate treatment should be implemented. However, in the vast majority of cases, no causes are found, and treatment is provided on a symptomatic basis. Treatment with antiviral agents has not proved to be any more effective in fatigue than placebo (Straus, Dale, Tobi, et al., 1988). Most professionals agree that the successful treatment of chronic fatigue syndrome should involve multiple approaches. It is essential to evaluate the coexistence of depression and to treat it with antidepressant medications and cognitive therapy. In addition, behavioral techniques may be utilized to alter the avoidant behavior that so often sustains the symptoms. Like patients with Somatoform Disorders, most patients with chronic fatigue syndrome will continue to seek medical evaluations and repeated diagnostic investigations despite negative results. It is essential to limit such medical interventions and to encourage the patient to pursue a course of rehabilitation rather than waste additional time and money.

Patients with chronic fatigue syndrome are often hostile toward psychological interventions and are very resistant to being referred for psychotherapy. Therefore, psychotherapeutic techniques should consist mainly of education, explanation, and encouragement of patients to be open-minded and to accept the possibility that the syn-

drome could be caused by both physical and psychological factors. Patients are encouraged to exercise, to gradually increase their level of physical activity, and to use
small gains to attain further improvement. Self-help
groups and other support organizations may be beneficial;
unfortunately, a patient's belief that he or she has a physical or a psychiatric disorder may be reinforced by other
patients, causing further complications and persistence of
symptoms (Kellner, 1991).

The fact that antidepressant medications seem to benefit
both chronic fatigue syndrome and Depressive Disorders
may suggest that both conditions are caused by similar
disturbances in brain neurochemistry. Goodnick and
Sandoval (1993) concluded that response to some antidepressants among patients with chronic fatigue syndrome
may occur at doses lower than those needed for the
treatment of major depression; for example, 25 to 75 mg of
amitriptyline (Elavil) per day is adequate to treat chronic
fatigue syndrome or fibromyalgia. Furthermore, they reported that antidepressant medications that possess high
serotonergic properties (e.g., Prozac, Elavil, and Anafranil)
were more effective in alleviating pain than depression,
whereas antidepressants with high catecholaminergic
properties (e.g., Wellbutrin and Ludiomil) seemed to be
more effective for symptoms associated with depression.
A combination of antidepressants may be used with caution in some patients.

COURSE AND PROGNOSIS

The prognosis of chronic fatigue syndrome varies considerably from one patient to another. In some patients, the
symptoms may be mild and short lived, as in patients
recovering from certain viral infections. However, in most
cases, the symptoms are severe and the syndrome may
linger for years. Treatments that combine psychiatric in-

terventions with rehabilitation programs seem to offer the best hope for improvement.

As in fibromyalgia, patients with chronic fatigue syndrome can become disabled and socially isolated due to fatigue, sleep disturbance, depression, and withdrawal. This may lead to significant disruptions in family and occupational aspects of life (Chapter 16).

18

PREMENSTRUAL SYNDROME

DEFINITION AND CLINICAL PRESENTATION

Premenstrual syndrome or PMS refers to a group of physical and psychological symptoms that occur in certain women prior to the onset of their menses and interfere with their normal routines. DSM-IV (1994) includes "Premenstrual Dysphoric Disorder" in the section of proposed categories that require further study, as there was not sufficient evidence to warrant its inclusion as an official disorder. The DSM-IV distinguishes between premenstrual syndrome and Premenstrual Dysphoric Disorder. It reserves the latter disorder for the more severe condition that interferes with work or social activities. DSM-IV considers premenstrual syndrome to be a much more common disorder than Premenstrual Dysphoric Disorder.

Symptoms vary from one woman to another and occur in variable degrees of severity and in different combinations. Essential features include depressive mood, marked anxiety, emotional instability, and irritability. Among other symptoms are episodes of angry outbursts, increased marital or other interpersonal conflicts, lack of interest in usual activities, fatigue, low energy level, poor concentration, binge eating or craving such foods as carbohydrates and salt, insomnia or hypersomnia, breast tenderness, headaches, sensation of bloating, joint or muscle pain,

and, occasionally, suicidal ideation. The symptoms seem
to commence during the week prior to the onset of menses,
begin to resolve a few days after the onset of menses and are
absent in the week following menses. The pattern of onset
and remission of the symptoms is repeated over several
months.

EPIDEMIOLOGY

It is estimated that at least 75 percent of women report
minor or sporadic premenstrual changes. Studies have
shown that variable degrees of premenstrual syndrome
occur in 20 percent to 50 percent of women studied;
however, only 3 percent to 5 percent of those women have
all of the symptoms included in the proposed criteria for
Premenstrual Dysphoric Disorder outlined in DSM-IV
(1994).

This disorder can begin at any age after menarche, and
seems to occur more commonly during the teens to late
20s. The symptoms may worsen with age and may vary
from cycle to cycle. Women who seek treatment are usually in their 30s. Symptoms are known to persist for a long
time and usually remit with the onset of menopause (DSM-
IV, 1994).

ETIOLOGY AND CONTRIBUTING FACTORS

No definitive etiology for premenstrual syndrome has
been identified. However, various hormonal and neurotransmitter systems are most likely to be responsible for
the condition. Certain research findings have identified
abnormalities in serotonin or melatonin secretion patterns
and abnormal sleep EEG findings among women with this
disorder. Other theories implicate vitamin B deficiency,
glucose metabolism, endorphins, and other systems (Droba
& Whybrow, 1989).

Women with a history of recurrent Mood Disorders or those with a family history of such disorders may be at greater risk for developing premenstrual syndrome (DSM-IV, 1994).

DIFFERENTIAL DIAGNOSIS

Due to the nature of this disorder, it is essential to differentiate it from a variety of psychiatric conditions that can be exacerbated during the premenstrual phase. These include Mood Disorders, Anxiety Disorders, Somatoform Disorders, bulimia nervosa, substance abuse, and Personality Disorders. These conditions are differentiated from premenstrual syndrome in that they persist throughout the cycle, among other diagnostic criteria. In addition, several medical conditions may present with similar features, such as seizure disorders, endocrine diseases, cancer, systemic lupus erythematosus, anemia, endometriosis, and various infections. Such medical conditions can be distinguished from Premenstrual Dysphoric Disorder by history, physical examination, and laboratory investigations (DSM-IV, 1994).

It is important to note here that women with preexisting Mood or Anxiety Disorders may report premenstrual exacerbation of their symptoms.

TREATMENT

The treatment of premenstrual syndrome can be difficult and frustrating and must involve the patient's participation and cooperation. Most symptoms can be treated symptomatically and may warrant the use of diuretics and painkillers. Hormonal treatment remains controversial (Moline, 1993). The use of progesterone and synthetic progesterone appears to be promising. Bromocriptine, prostaglandin inhibitors, and vitamin B_6 have also been helpful in some patients (Droba & Whybrow, 1989).

Supportive psychotherapy may help. In addition, the use of various psychotropic medications has proved to be very beneficial (Pariser, 1993). Anxiolytic agents, lithium, and antidepressants, particularly the new serotonin reuptake inhibitors (such as Prozac, Zoloft, and Paxil), can be of definite value.

PROGNOSIS

Premenstrual syndrome appears to worsen with age, especially in women in their 30s and 40s. The symptoms resolve gradually with the onset of menopause. The illness can be severe enough to seriously interfere with the woman's social and occupational life. Job problems and marital conflicts are frequent complications. Treatment consisting of medical and psychological interventions offers good results and improves the prognosis sufficiently to minimize the syndrome's impact on the functioning of the patient.

19

FUTURE DIRECTION OF PSYCHOSOMATIC MEDICINE

In the early decades of the 20th century and following the insight of Freud who brought the psyche and the soma back together, a number of researchers and clinicians attempted to expand the understanding of the dynamic relationship between the mind and the body. Theories were suggested by various authors focusing on specific emotions, conflicts, stress, and personality organizations as primary factors in psychosomatic pathology. Franz Alexander (1891–1964) led that movement and made significant contributions to the field of psychosomatic medicine. The theories presented by Franz and others, while interesting and perhaps relevant, generated controversy among experts in both medicine and psychiatry. The lack of scientific proof behind such theories has caused the enthusiasm about Psychosomatic Disorders to diminish in the past two decades. Instead, a tremendous interest has been generated in the fields of psychoneurobiology and psychoimmunology. Recent research has been able to redefine the connection between the psyche and the soma utilizing more scientifically convincing hypotheses. It has become possible for some consensus to be reached regarding the role of emotional stress in physical illness as a result of changes in the endocrine and immune systems. Conversely, it has been shown that physical illness can lead to emotional changes by influencing the neurotransmitter systems within the brain. It is now possible to tell a patient with premenstrual syndrome, for example, that her irritability and mood swings are due to alterations in various neurotransmitter systems caused by fluctuations in the hormonal balance. It is also clear to a hypertensive patient that emotional stress can increase his or her blood pressure through the release of excessive amounts of catecholamines.

During this "Decade of the Brain," so proclaimed by former President George Bush, new discoveries utilizing technologically advanced diagnostic procedures and ongoing research in psychopharmacology will undoubtedly continue to narrow the gap between physical illness and emotional illness. It is not unlikely that soon specific emotions and behaviors such as guilt, anger, and love will be explained by simple chemical processes in the brain. Even ego functions and defenses will be accounted for by brain neurochemistry. In essence, the mind will not just be seen as connected to the body, but the two will be viewed as one dynamic entity.

In this era of health care reforms and managed care, early recognition and treatment of certain Somatoform Disorders and Psychosomatic Disorders is extremely important. A patient with Somatization Disorder or Conversion Disorder, for example, may undergo highly expensive diagnostic procedures unnecessarily before the real diagnosis is recognized and addressed appropriately. Similarly, inappropriate medical care can be avoided if patients with Panic Disorder are identified and treated effectively instead of going through repeated cardiological examinations and expensive procedures. Mental health professionals are much better equipped than other health care providers to identify and treat such patients. Mental health providers will hold an increasingly important, if not critical position, in order that health care be delivered efficiently and effectively. The stigma of mental illness will undoubtedly disappear as the functioning of the mind is better understood in "medical" terms, and as the mind more and more is viewed as a most integral part of the body as opposed to a separate entity. This evolution in perspective should facilitate the acceptance and natural inclusion of mental health providers on the health care team.

REFERENCES

Alexander, F. (1950). *Psychosomatic medicine: Its principles and applications.* New York: Norton.

Allison, D. B., & Heshka, S. (1993). Emotion and eating in obesity? A critical analysis. *International Journal of Eating Disorders, 13*(3), 289–295.

American Psychiatric Association (1994). *Diagnostic and statistical manual of mental disorders* (4th ed.). Washington, DC: Author.

Andrasik, F. (1990). Psychologic and behavioral aspects of chronic headaches. *Neurologic Clinics, 8*(4), 961–976.

Asaad, G. (1990). *Hallucinations in clinical psychiatry: A guide for mental health professionals.* New York: Brunner/Mazel.

Asaad, G. (1995). *Understanding mental disorders due to medical conditions or substance abuse: What every therapist should know.* New York: Brunner/Mazel.

Blackwell, B., Merskey, H., & Kellner, R. (1989). Somatoform pain disorders. In *Treatment of psychiatric disorders, Vol. 3.* Washington, DC: American Psychiatric Press.

Bray, G. A. (1978). Definitions, measurements and classification of the syndromes of obesity. *International Journal of Obesity, 2,* 99–112.

Breslau, N. (1992). Migraine, suicidal ideation, and suicide attempts. *Neurology, 42*(2), 392–395.

Brown, S. R., Schwartz, J. M., Summergrad, P., et al. (1986). Globus hystericus syndrome responsive to antidepressants. *American Journal of Psychiatry, 143,* 917–918.

Buchwald, D., & Garrity, D. (1994). Comparison of patients with chronic fatigue syndrome, fibromyalgia, and multiple chemical sensitivities. *Archives of Internal Medicine, 154*(18), 2049–2053.

Burns, B. H., & Howell, J. B. L. (1969). Disproportionately severe breathlessness in chronic bronchitis. *Quarterly Journal of Medicine, 38,* 277–294.

Burns, R. W., Kellum, W. C., Bienvenu, L., et al. (1985). Esophageal motor disorders and atypical chest pain: Long-term clinical follow-up [abstract]. *American Journal of Gastroenterology, 80,* 833A.

Chapman, C. R., & Turner, J. A. (1990). Psychologic and psychosocial aspects of acute pain. In J. J. Bonica (Ed.), *The management of pain, Vol. I,* (2nd ed.). Philadelphia: Lea & Febiger.

Christensen, L. (1993). Effects of eating behavior on mood: A review of the literature. *International Journal of Eating Disorders, 14*(2), 171–183.

Clouse, R. E. (1992). Psychiatric interactions with the esophagus. *Psychiatric Annals, 22,* 598–605.

De Leon, J., Bott, A., & Simpson, G. M. (1989). Dysmorphophobia: Body dysmorphic disorder or delusional disorder, somatic subtype? *Comprehensive Psychiatry, 30,* 457–472.

Droba, M., & Whybrow, P. C. (1989). Endocrine and metabolic disorders. In H. I. Kaplan & B. J. Sadock (Eds.), *Comprehensive textbook of psychiatry* (5th ed.). Baltimore: Williams & Wilkins.

Eisendrath, S. J. (1989). Factitious disorder with physical symptoms. In *Treatment of psychiatric disorders, Vol. 3.* Washington, DC: American Psychiatric Press.

Engels, W. D. (1985). Skin disorders. In H. I. Kaplan & B. J. Sadock (Eds.), *Comprehensive textbook of psychiatry* (4th ed.). Baltimore: Williams & Wilkins.

Fawzy, F. I., Cousins, N., Fawzy, N. W., et al. (1990). A structured psychiatric intervention for cancer patients, I: Changes over time in methods of coping and affective disturbance. *Archives of General Psychiatry, 47,* 720–725.

Fawzy, F. I., Kemeny, M. E., Fawzy, N. W., et al. (1990). A structured psychiatric intervention for cancer patients, II: Changes over time in immunological measures. *Archives of General Psychiatry, 47,* 729–735.

Ferraccioli, G., Ghirelli, L., Scita, F., et al. (1987). EMG-biofeedback training in fibromyalgia syndrome. *Journal of Rheumatology, 14,* 820–825.

Fine, P. G., Milano, R., & Hard, B. D. (1988). The effects of myofascial trigger point injections are naloxone reversible. *Pain, 32,* 15–20.

Fisher, P., Greenwood, A., Huskisson, E. C., et al. (1989). Effect of homeopathic treatment on fibrositis (primary fibromyalgia). *British Medical Journal, 299,* 365–366.

Folks, D. G., & Freeman, A. M. (1985). Munchausen's syndrome and other factitious illness. *Psychiatric Clinics of North America, 8,* 263–278.

Ford, C. V. (1983). *The somatizing disorders—Illness as a way of life.* New York: Elsevier Biomedical.

Garvey, M. J., and Tollefson, G. D. (1988). Association of affective disorder with migraine headaches and neurodermatitis. *General Hospital Psychiatry, 10,* 148–149.

Geyer, S. (1991). Life events prior to manifestation of breast cancer: A limited prospective study covering eight years before diagnosis. *Journal of Psychosomatic Research, 35,* 355–363.

Glover, V., Jarman, J., & Sandler, M. (1993). Migraine and depression: Biological aspects. *Journal of Psychiatric Research, 27(2),* 223–231.

Goldenberg, D. L. (1986). Psychological studies in fibrositis. *American Journal of Medicine, 81,* 67–70.

Goodnick, P. J., & Sandoval, R. (1993). Psychotropic treatment of chronic fatigue syndrome and related disorders. *Journal of Clinical Psychiatry, 54,* 13–20.

Gorman, J. M., & Kertzner, R. (1990). Psychoneuroimmunology and HIV infection. *Journal of Neuropsychiatry and Clinical Neurosciences, 2,* 241–252.

Gray, L. P. (1983). The relationship of the "inferior constrictor swallow" and "globus hystericus" or the hypopharyngeal syndrome. *Journal of Laryngology and Otology, 97,* 607–618.

Greenberg, D. B., Stern, T. A., & Weilburg, J. B. (1988). The fear of choking: Three successfully treated cases. *Psychosomatics, 29,* 126–129.

Greer, S., Morris, T., & Pettingale, K. W. (1979). Psychological response to breast cancer: Effect on outcome. *Lancet, 2,* 785–787.

Hackett, T. P., Rosenbaum, J. F., & Cassem, N. H. (1985). Cardiovascular disorders. In H. I. Kaplan & B. J. Sadock (Eds.), *Comprehensive textbook of psychiatry* (4th ed.). Baltimore: Williams & Wilkins.

Halmi, K. A. (1994). Eating disorders: Anorexia nervosa, bulimia nervosa, and obesity. In R. E. Hales, S. C. Yudofsky, & J. A. Talbott (Eds.), *The American psychiatric press textbook of psychiatry* (2nd ed.). Washington, DC: American Psychiatric Press.

Harvey, R. F., Mauad, E. C., & Brown, A. M. (1987). Prognosis in the irritable bowel syndrome: A 5-year prospective study. *Lancet, 1,* 963–965.

Holmes, G. P., Kaplan, J. E., Gantz, N. M., et al. (1988). Chronic fatigue syndrome: A working case definition. *Annals of Internal Medicine, 108,* 387–389.

Irwin, M., Daniel, S., Smith, T. L., et al. (1987). Impaired natural killer cell activity during bereavement. *Brain, Behavior and Immunology, 1,* 98–104.

Kellner, R. (1989). Hypochondriasis and body dysmorphic disorder. In *Treatment of psychiatric disorders, Vol. 3.* Washington, DC: American Psychiatric Association.

Kellner, R. (1991). *Psychosomatic syndromes and somatic symptoms.* Washington, DC: American Psychiatric Press.

King, S. A., & Strain, J. (1994). Pain disorders. In R. E. Hales, S. C. Yudofsky, & J. A. Talbott (Eds.), *The American psychiatric press textbook of psychiatry* (2nd ed.). Washington, DC: American Psychiatric Press.

Knapp, P. (1985). Current theoretical concepts in psychosomatic medicine. In H. I. Kaplan & B. J. Sadock (Eds.), *Comprehensive textbook of psychiatry* (4th ed.). Baltimore: Williams & Wilkins.

Krag, N. J., Norregaard, J., Larsen, J. K., et al. (1994). A blinded, controlled evaluation of anxiety and depressive symptoms in patients with fibromyalgia, as measured by standardized psychometric interview scales. *Acta Psychiatrica Scandinavica, 89,* 370–375.

Lydiard, R. B. (1992). Anxiety and the irritable bowel syndrome. *Psychiatric Annals, 22,* 612–618.

Manu, P., Matthews, D. A., & Lane, T. J. (1988). The mental health patient with a chief complaint of chronic fatigue. *Archives of Internal Medicine, 148,* 2213–2217.

Martin, R. L., Yutzy, S. H. (1994). Somatoform disorders. In R. E. Hales, S. C. Yudofsky, & J. A. Talbott (Eds.), *The American psychiatric press textbook of psychiatry* (2nd ed.). Washington, DC: American Psychiatric Press.

Masi, A. T., & Yunus, M. B. (1986). Concepts of illness in populations as applied to fibromyalgia syndrome. *American Journal of Medicine, 81* (Suppl. 3A), 19–25.

McCain, G. A. (1989). Nonmedical treatments in primary fibromyalgia. *Rheumatic Diseases Clinics of North America, 15,* 73–90.

McDaniel, J. S., Moran, M. G., Levenson, J. L., & Stoudemire, A. (1994). Psychological factors affecting medical conditions. In R. E. Hales, S. C. Yudofsky, & J. A. Talbott (Eds.), *The American psychiatric press textbook of psychiatry* (2nd ed.). Washington, DC: American Psychiatric Press.

Merskey, H. (1979). *The analysis of hysteria.* London: Bailliere Tindall.

Merskey, H. (1986). Classification of chronic pain. *Pain,* (Suppl. 3), S1–S226.

Merskey, H. (1989). Conversion disorders. In *Treatment of Psychiatric Disorders, Vol. 3.* Washington, DC: American Psychiatric Association.

Moline, M. L. (1993). Pharmacologic strategies for managing premenstrual syndrome. *Clinical Pharmacology, 12,* 181–196.

North, C. S., Alpers, D. H., Helzer, J. E., et al. (1991). Do life events or depression exacerbate inflammatory bowel disease? A prospective study. *Annals of Internal Medicine, 114,* 381–386.

Olden, K. W. (1992). Inflammatory bowel disease: A biopsychosocial perspective. *Psychiatric Annals, 22,* 619–623.

O'Neil, P. M., & Jarrell, M. P. (1992). Psychological aspects of obesity and very-low-calorie diets. *American Journal of Clinical Nutrition, 56* (Suppl. 1), 185S–189S.

Oparic, S. (1992). Arterial hypertension. In J. B. Wyngaarden, L. H. Smith, Jr., & J. C. Bennett (Eds.), *Cecil textbook of medicine* (19th ed.). Philadelphia: W. B. Saunders.

Osterweis, M., Kleinman, A., & Mechanic, D. (Eds.). (1987). *Pain and disability.* Washington, DC: National Academy Press.

Pariser, S. F. (1993). Women and mood disorders: Menarche to menopause. *Annals of Clinical Psychiatry,* 5, 249–254.

Passchier, J., Schouten, J., Van-der-Donk, J., & Van-Romunde, L. K. (1991). The association of frequent headaches with personality and life events. *Headache, 31*(2), 116–121.

Phillips, K. A., McElroy, S. L., Keck, P. E., Jr., et al. (1993). Body dysmorphic disorder: 30 cases of imagined ugliness. *American Journal of Psychiatry, 150,* 302–308.

Plewes, J. M., & Fagan, J. G. (1994). Factitious disorders and malingering. In R. E. Hales, S. C. Yudofsky, & J. A. Talbott (Eds.), *The American psychiatric press textbook of psychiatry* (2nd ed.). Washington, DC: American Psychiatric Press.

Pope, H. G., Jr., Jonas, J. M., & Jones, B. (1982). Factitious psychosis: Phenomenology, family history, and long-term outcome of nine patients. *American Journal of Psychiatry, 139,* 1480–1483.

Ramsay, B., & O'Reagan, M. (1988). A survey of the social and psychological effects of psoriasis. *British Journal of Dermatology, 118,* 195–201.

Rubinow, D. R., Peck, G. L., Squillace, K. M., et al. (1987). Reduced anxiety and depression in cystic acne patients after successful treatment with oral isotretinoin. *Journal of the American Academy of Dermatology, 17,* 25–32.

Sharma, S., & Nandkumar, V. K. (1980). Personality structure and adjustment pattern in bronchial asthma. *Acta Psychiatrica Scandinavica, 61,* 81–88.

Shekelle, R. B., Raynor, W. J., & Ostfeld, A. M. (1981). Psychological depression and 17-year risk of death from cancer. *Psychosomatic Medicine, 43,* 117–125.

Shulman, B. H. (1991). Psychiatric aspects of headache. *Medical Clinics of North America, 75*(3), 707–715.

Slater, E. (1965). The diagnosis of hysteria. *British Medical Journal, 1,* 1395–1399.

Smith, G. R., Monson, R. A., & Ray, D. C. (1986). Psychiatric consultation in somatization disorder. *New England Journal of Medicine, 314,* 1407–1413.

Solyom, L., & Sookman, D. (1980). Fear of choking and its treatment. *Canadian Journal of Psychiatry, 25,* 30–34

Spiegel, D., Bloom, J. R., Kramer, H. C., et al. (1989). Effect of psychosocial treatment on survival of patients with metastatic breast cancer. *Lancet, 2,* 888–891.

Stein, M., Miller, A. H., & Trestman, R. L. (1991). Depression, the immune system, and health and illness: Findings in search of meaning. *Archives of General Psychiatry, 48,* 171–177.

Stone, M. H. (1977). Factitious illness: Psychological findings and treatment recommendations. *Bulletin of the Menninger Clinic, 41,* 239–254.

Straus, S. E., Dale, J. K., Tobi, M., et al. (1988). Acyclovir treatment of the chronic fatigue syndrome. *New England Journal of Medicine, 319,* 1692–1698.

Van Putten, T., & Alban, J. (1977). Lithium carbonate in personality disorders: A case of hysteria. *Journal of Nervous and Mental Disorders, 164,* 218–222.

Yap, P. M. (1965). Koro: A culture-bound depersonalization syndrome. *British Journal of Psychiatry, 111,* 43.

Yunus, M. B. (1989). Fibromyalgia syndrome: New research on an old malady. *British Medical Journal, 298,* 474–475.

NAME INDEX

Alban, J., 51
Alexander, F., 69, 97, 129
Allison, D. B., 109
Alpers, D. H., 74
Andrasik, F., 10,
Asaad, G., ix, xii, 16, 56

Bienvenu, L., 68
Blackwell, B., 40, 41
Bloom, J. R., 99
Bott, A., 27
Bray, G. A., 107
Breslau, N., 105
Brown, A. M., 73
Brown, S. R., 67
Buchwald, D., 113, 117, 119, 120
Burns, B. H., 86
Burns, R. W., 68

Chapman, C. R., 37
Christensen, L., 109
Clouse, R. E., 66, 67, 68
Cousins, N., 99

Dale, J. K., 121
Daniel, S., 96

De Leon, J., 27, 28
Droba, M., 126, 127

Eisendrath, S. J., 48, 50
Engels, W. D., 92, 93, 94

Fagan, J. G., 50, 51
Fawzy, F. I., 99
Fawzy, N. W., 99
Ferraccioli, G., 116
Fine, P. G., 116
Fisher, P., 116
Folks, D. G., 48
Ford, C. V., 50
Freeman, A. M., 48
Freud, ix, 129
Gantz, N. M., 119
Garrity, D., 113, 117, 119, 120
Garvey, M. J., 92
Geyer, S., 98
Ghirelli, L., 116
Glover, V., 102
Goldenberg, D. L., 115
Goodnick, P. J., 122
Gorman, J. M., 96
Gray, L. P., 68

Greenberg, D. B., 67
Greenwood, A., 116
Greer, S., 98

Hackett, T. P., 80
Halmi, K. A., 107, 108, 110, 111
Hard, B. D., 116
Harvey, R. F., 73
Heshka, S., 109
Helzer, J. E., 74
Holmes, G. P., 119, 120
Howell, J. B. L., 86
Huskisson, E. C., 116

Irwin, M., 96

Jarman, J., 102
Jarrell, M. P., 109
Jonas, J. M., 49
Jones, B., 49

Kaplan, J. E., 119
Keck, P. E., Jr., 32
Kellner, R., 6, 14, 15, 16, 21, 25,
    26, 40, 62, 66, 67, 69, 70,
    72, 87, 113, 114, 115, 120,
    122
Kellum, W. C., 68
Kemeny, M. E., 99
Kertzner, R., 96
King, S. A., 35, 39
Kleinman, A., 33
Knapp, P., 96, 98
Krag, N. J., 114
Kramer, H. C., 99

Lane, T. J., 120
Larsen, J. K., 114
Levenson, J. L., 70
Lydiard, R. B., 71

Manu, P., 120
Martin, R. L., 19, 23, 26, 30, 32
Masi, A. T., 117
Matthews, D. A., 120
Mauad, E. C., 73

McCain, G. A., 117
McDaniel, J. S., 70, 72, 78, 80,
    84, 86, 96, 97, 99
McElroy, S. L., 32
Mechanic, D., 33
Merskey, H., 12, 14, 17, 33, 40,
    54
Milano, R., 116
Miller, A. H., 96
Moline, M. L., 127
Monson, R. A., 10
Moran, M. G., 70
Morris, T., 98

Nandkumar, V. K., 84
Norregaard, J., 114
North, C. S., 74

Olden, K. W., 74
O'Neil, P. M., 109
Oparic, S., 78
O'Reagan, M., 92
Osterweis, M., 33
Ostfeld, A. M., 99

Pariser, S. F., 128
Passchier, J., 103
Peck, G. L., 93
Pettingale, K. W., 99
Phillips, K. A., 32
Plewes, J. M., 50, 51
Pope, H. G., Jr., 49

Ramsay, B., 92
Ray, D. C., 10
Raynor, W. J., 99
Rubinow, D. R., 93

Sandler, M., 102
Sandoval, R., 122
Schouten, J., 103
Schwartz, J. M., 67
Scita, F., 116
Sharma, S., 84
Shekelle, R. B., 99
Shulman, B. H., 103, 104
Simpson, G. M., 27

Slater, E., 14
Smith, G. R., 10
Smith, T. L., 96
Solyom, L., 67
Sookman, D., 67
Spiegel, D., 99
Squillace, K. M., 93
Stein, M., 96
Stern, T. A., 67
Stone, M. H., 50
Stoudemire, A., 70
Strain, J., 35, 39
Straus, S. E., 121
Summergrad, P., 67

Tobi, M., 139
Tollefson, G. D., 92
Trestman, R. L., 96
Turner, J. A., 37

Van-der-Donk, J., 103
Van Putten, T., 51
Van-Romunde, L. K., 103

Weilburg, J. B., 67
Whybrow, P. C., 126, 127

Yap, P. M., 31
Yunus, M. B., 113, 117
Yutzy, S. H., 19, 23, 26, 30, 32

SUBJECT INDEX

Acne, 93
Acupuncture, 40, 117
Aerophagia, 70
Alexithyymia, 7, 70
Alopecia Areata, 94
Asthma, Bronchial, 83–85

Biofeedback, 39–40
Body Dysmorphic Disorder,
    27–32
  associated features, 28–29
  case example, 29
  clinical features, 27
  course, 32
  definition, 27
  diagnosis, 30–31
  differential diagnosis,
    30–31
  etiology, 30
  prognosis, 32
  treatment, 31–32
Bronchitis, chronic, 85

Cardiovascular Disorders,
    77–81
Chronic Fatigue, 119

Chronic Fatigue Syndrome,
    119–123
Chronic Obstructive Pulmonary
    Disease (COPD), 85–87
Conversion Disorder, 11–18
  associated features, 12
  case examples, 12–14
  clinical presentation, 11–12
  course, 17–18
  definition, 11
  diagnosis, 15–16
  differential diagnosis, 15–17
  etiology, 14–15
  prognosis, 17–18
  subtypes, 11–12
  treatment, 17
Coronary Artery Disease, 79–81
Crohn's Disease, see Regional
    Enteritis

Delta Sleep-inducing Neuropep-
    tides (DSLP), 41
Dermatitis, Atopic, 92
Dermatological Disorders, 91–94
Dysmorphophobia, see Body
    Dysmorphic Disorder

Dyspepsia, 68–71
Dysphagia, 65–68

Eczema, 92
Emphysema, 85

Factitious Disorder by Proxy,
    51–52
Factitious Disorder with
    Physical Signs and Symp-
    toms, 45–52
  associated features, 46
  case example, 47–48
  clinical presentation, 45–46
  course, 51
  definition, 45
  diagnosis, 49–50
  differential diagnosis, 49–50
  etiology, 48
  prognosis, 51
  treatment, 50–51
Factitious Disorder with
    Psychological Signs and
    Symptoms, 53–57
  associated features, 54
  case example, 54–55
  clinical presentation, 53–54
  course, 57
  definition, 53
  diagnosis, 56–57
  differential diagnosis, 56–57
  etiology, 55–56
  prognosis, 57
  treatment, 57
Fear of Choking, 65–68
Fibromyalgia, 113–117
Fibrositis, *see* Fibromyalgia

Ganser's Syndrome, 54
Gastrointestinal Disorders, 65–75
Globus (globus hystericus), 65–68

Headaches, 101–105
  migraine, 102
  posttraumatic, 101–102
  tension, 101

Hypertension, 78–79
Hyperventilation Syndrome,
    87–89
Hypnosis, 40
Hypopchondriasis, 19–26
  associated features, 20–21
  case example, 21–22
  clinical presentation, 19–20
  course, 26
  definition, 19
  diagnosis, 23–24
  differential diagnosis, 23–24
  etiology, 22–23
  prognosis, 26
  treatment, 25–26
Hysteria, *see* Conversion
    Disorder
Hysterical Psychosis, 54

Inflammatory Bowel Disease,
    73–75
Irritable Bowel Syndrome, 71–73

Koro, 31

Low-power Laser Irradiation,
    41

Malingering, 59–62
  associated features, 60
  case example, 60
  clinical presentation, 59
  course, 62
  definition, 59
  diagnosis, 61–62
  differential diagnosis, 61–62
  etiology, 61
  prognosis, 62
  treatment, 62
Migraine, 101–105
Munchausen's Syndrome, 45.
    See also Factitious Disorder
    with Physical Signs and
    Symptoms
Munchausen's Syndrome by
    Proxy, 51–52

Nerve Block, 40
Neurasthenia, 121

Obesity, 107–112

Pain Disorder, 33–42
  associated features, 35
  case example, 35–36
  clinical presentation, 33–34
  course, 41–42
  definition, 33
  diagnosis, 37–38
  diagnostic criteria, 34
  differential diagnosis,
    37–38
  etiology, 37
  management, 38–41
  prognosis, 41–42
  subtypes, 34–35
Peptic Ulcer, 68–71
Posthypnotic suggestion, 40
Premenstrual Syndrome,
  125–128
Pruritus, 93–94
Pseudodysphagia, *see* Fear of
  Choking
Pseudologia Fantastica, 49,
  56
Pseudoseizures, 12, 16
Psoriasis, 92
Psychoimmunology, 95–97

Psychooncology, 97–100
Regional Enteritis, 73–75
Relaxation technique, 39–40
Respiratory Disorders,
  83–89
Rheumatoid Arthritis, 97

Somatization Disorder, 3–10
  associated features, 4–5
  case example, 5–6
  clinical presentation, 3–4
  course, 10
  definition, 3–4
  diagnostic criteria, 4
  differential diagnosis, 7–8
  etiology, 6–7
  prognosis, 10
  treatment, 9–10
Spastic Colitis, *see* Irritable
  Bowel Syndrome

Transcutaneous Electrical
  Nerve Stimulation (TENS),
  40, 117
Trigger Point Injection, 40
Type A personality, 70, 80

Ulcerative Colitis, 73–75
Undifferentiated Somatoform
  Disorder, 9
Urticaria, 93